Love is friendship that has caught fire. It is quiet understanding, mutual confidence, sharing and forgiving. It is loyalty through good and bad times. It settles for less than perfection and makes allowances for human weaknesses.

Ann Landers

To succeed in life, you need two things: ignorance and confidence.

Mark Twain

Believe in yourself! Have faith in your abilities! Without a humble but reasonable confidence in your own powers you cannot be successful or happy.

Norman Vincent Peale

Optimism is the faith that leads to achievement. Nothing can be done without hope and confidence.

Helen Keller

Kindness in words creates confidence. Kindness in thinking creates profoundness. Kindness in giving creates love.

Lao Tzu

Leadership is solving problems. The day soldiers stop bringing you their problems is the day you have stopped leading them. They have either lost confidence that you can help or concluded you do not care. Either case is a failure of leadership.

Colin Powell

We gain strength, and courage, and confidence by each experience in which we really stop to look fear in the face... we must do that which we think we cannot.

Eleanor Roosevelt

You gain strength, courage, and confidence by every experience in which you really stop to look fear in the face. You are able to say to yourself, 'I lived through this horror. I can take the next thing that comes along.'

Eleanor Roosevelt

When you have confidence, you can have a lot of fun. And when you have fun, you can do amazing things.

Joe Namath

Life is not easy for any of us. But what of that? We must have perseverance and above all confidence in ourselves. We must believe that we are gifted for something and that this thing must be attained.

Marie Curie

Fear stifles our thinking and actions. It creates indecisiveness that results in stagnation. I have known talented people who procrastinate indefinitely rather than risk failure. Lost opportunities cause erosion of confidence, and the downward spiral begins.

Charles Stanley

With confidence, you have won before you have started.

Marcus Garvey

When a team outgrows individual performance and learns team confidence, excellence becomes a reality.

Joe Paterno

I have always loved fashion because it's a great way to express your mood. And I'm definitely a shoe lover. The right pair of shoes can change the feel of an outfit, and even change how a woman feels about herself. A woman can wear confidence on her feet with a high stiletto, or slip into weekend comfort with a soft ballet flat.

Fergie

Ignorance more frequently begets confidence than does knowledge: it is those who know little, and not those who know much, who so positively assert that this or that problem will never be solved by science.

Charles Darwin

Find your self-respect now. Don't dumb yourselves down. Think of yourself as capable and worthy of finding a guy who is going to respect you, too. It's so important, I mean, and the confidence you get from feeling smart and tackling something like mathematics, which is a challenge, right? Math is hard.

Danica McKellar

Be courteous to all, but intimate with few, and let those few be well tried before you give them your confidence.

George Washington

If you have no confidence in self, you are twice defeated in the race of life.

Marcus Garvey

Confidence... thrives on honesty, on honor, on the sacredness of obligations, on faithful protection and on unselfish performance. Without them it cannot live.

Franklin D. Roosevelt

Inaction breeds doubt and fear. Action breeds confidence and courage. If you want to conquer fear, do not sit home and think about it. Go out and get busy.

Dale Carnegie

Have no fear of moving into the unknown. Simply step out fearlessly knowing that I am with you, therefore no harm can befall you; all is very, very well. Do this in complete faith and confidence.

Pope John Paul II

Confidence has nothing to do with what you look like. If you obsess over that, you'll end up being disappointed in yourself all the time. Instead, high self-esteem comes from how you feel in any moment. So walk into a room acting like you're in charge, and spend your energy on making the people around you happy.

Marian Seldes

Confidence comes from discipline and training.

Robert Kiyosaki

If you're presenting yourself with confidence, you can pull off pretty much anything.

Katy Perry

Sometimes we may ask God for success, and He gives us physical and mental stamina. We might plead for prosperity, and we receive enlarged perspective and increased patience, or we petition for growth and are blessed with the gift of grace. He may bestow upon us conviction and confidence as we strive to achieve worthy goals.

David A. Bednar

Looking at America's history, ordinary people did something extraordinary. Leaders risked their lives for freedoms that we take for granted today.That's what instills confidence. That's us. We will move forward and prosper because that's who we are as Americans.

Scott Walker

Most athletes are media shy. They keep to themselves and to their training. I'm not saying it is absolutely necessary for them to come out and face the cameras with confidence, but if they do, it will only help them. They will find themselves closer to their fans and will also get their word across more effectively.

Vijender Singh

You need to develop, somehow, a huge amount of faith and confidence in yourself, because there's a lot of rejection throughout an actor's life and you have to believe in yourself more than anyone else.

Stephen Collins

A good 80 percent of the vault is still physical and another percentage of it, 20, 25 percent is mental. Mental is always the mental strength, the confidence building up to that contest or repetition, practice, practice, and practice.

Bela Karolyi

I was born with confidence in myself and who I am. Even when I was a little kid, I felt that, and I carried it all through my years. I'm 26 now, and I'm still that person. I think every woman needs to have that self-love.

Ricki-Lee Coulter

Thank you for the confidence put in my by the motherland and the people, for giving me this chance to represent China's millions of women by going into space.

Liu Yang

You always get things that teach you and steps to grow, but there is a confidence that is gained and a deep understanding of what it means to be supported by your knowledge - not by some team that is there to create confidence; it is there within you. That takes time. That takes teachers. That takes taking risks.

Sharon Lawrence

There is no country in the world with the diversity, confidence and talent and black pride like Nigeria.

Binyavanga Wainaina

I don't even know how to speak up for myself, because I don't really have a father who would give me the confidence or advice.

Eminem

All wars signify the failure of conflict resolution mechanisms, and they need post-war rebuilding of faith, trust and confidence.

A. P. J. Abdul Kalam

We do not so much need the help of our friends as the confidence of their help in need.

Epicurus

Confidence contributes more to conversation than wit.

Francois de La Rochefoucauld

There can be no great courage where there is no confidence or assurance, and half the battle is in the conviction that we can do what we undertake.

Orison Swett Marden

As is our confidence, so is our capacity.

William Hazlitt

Attempt easy tasks as if they were difficult, and difficult as if they were easy; in the one case that confidence may not fall asleep, in the other that it may not be dismayed.

Baltasar Gracian

Most of the confidence which I appear to feel, especially when influenced by noon wine, is only a pretense.

Tennessee Williams

I don't doubt for a second that Neil Armstrong's spirit is still with us: that unique blend of optimism, humility and the utter confidence that when the world needs someone to do the really big stuff, you need an American.

Mitt Romney

The words spoken by the leader of the free world can expand the frontiers of freedom or shrink them. When Ronald Reagan called on Gorbachev to 'tear down this wall,' a surge of confidence rose that would ultimately breach the bounds of the evil empire.

Mitt Romney

Every man who attacks my belief, diminishes in some degree my confidence in it, and therefore makes me uneasy; and I am angry with him who makes me uneasy.

Samuel Johnson

Confidence cannot find a place wherein to rest in safety.

Virgil

I was always looking outside myself for strength and confidence but it comes from within. It is there all the time.

Anna Freud

For peace is not mere absence of war, but is a virtue that springs from, a state of mind, a disposition for benevolence, confidence, justice.

Baruch Spinoza

Our most tragic error may have been our inability to establish a rapport and a confidence with the press and television with the communication media. I don't think the press has understood me.

Lyndon B. Johnson

Confidence is something you're born with. I know I had loads of it even at the age of 15.

Hedy Lamarr

People spending more of their own money on routine health care would make the system more competitive and transparent and restore the confidence between the patients and the doctors without government rationing.

Benjamin Carson

The methods and tools of science perennially breach barriers, granting me confidence that our epic march of insight into the operations of nature will continue without end.

Neil deGrasse Tyson

I have always felt strongly about empowering women. I'm living proof that, with confidence and by believing in yourself, you can accomplish any goal.

Queen Latifah

Religion is the possibility of the removal of every ground of confidence except confidence in God alone.

Karl Barth

I have so much confidence in the reality of Jesus that I feel no pressure to try to make people act or be a certain way. I'm banking everything on the fact that God actually changes people.

Erwin McManus

It is an honor and a privilege to be of service and support; however, I realize people are not putting their confidence in me. Instead, they are actually learning to trust themselves. My job is to affirm and support them in the process and teach them to do what I do when I need strength: I begin within.

Iyanla Vanzant

A big ego means that you have some confidence in your abilities, really, and that you're prepared to take the risk of trying them out.

Brian Eno

I actually think that the economy has got some positives. It's got the market. It's got consumer confidence and it's got banks throwing - I mean central bankers throwing money at it around the world.

Jack Welch

Perhaps a child who is fussed over gets a feeling of destiny; he thinks he is in the world for something important, and it gives him drive and confidence.

Benjamin Spock

History keeps her secrets longer than most of us. But she has one secret that I will reveal to you tonight in the greatest confidence. Sometimes there are no winners at all. And sometimes nobody needs to lose.

John le Carre

When a woman reaches twenty-six in America, she's on the slide. It's downhill all the way from then on. It doesn't give you a tremendous feeling of confidence and well-being.

Lauren Bacall

Men secretly respect a woman who is strong, has confidence and has dreams of her own. There's nothing more attractive to a man than a woman who has dignity and pride in who she is.

Sherry Argov

It's the government's job to encourage entrepreneurialism and investment. Most importantly, it's the government's duty to inspire confidence.

Simon Cowell

The die is set and Malcolm will not escape for the foolish talk he spoke against his benefactor, such a man, is worthy of death, and it would have been so, were it not for Muhammad's confidence that God would give him the victory over the enemies.

Louis Farrakhan

With a novelist, like a surgeon, you have to get a feeling that you've fallen into good hands - someone from whom you can accept the anesthetic with confidence.

Saul Bellow

I think all girls in the world wish they were a Parisian girl - that sort of effortless chic confidence and comfort in their own skin.

Natalie Portman

I think the most important thing that I think everyone in America must have is belief that wherever they live, whatever station they have in life, that the American dream is alive and well. I think the fracturing of trust and confidence is in the American dream.

Howard Schultz

I want to thank my parents for somehow raising me to have confidence that is disproportionate with my looks and abilities.

Tina Fey

I am consumed with the fear of failing. Reaching deep down and finding confidence has made all my dreams come true.

Arsenio Hall

Life is not quantifiable in terms of age, but I suppose in my fifties I am more grounded and more at ease in my own skin than when I was younger. I have a confidence that I didn't have before from the experiences I've had.

Annie Lennox

What I say on a record and what I say off a record is two different things. And that's always been the case. There's a difference between confidence on a record and arrogance.

LL Cool J

Climate change is the 800-pound gorilla in the living room

that the media dances around. But in the scientific community, it's a settled question: 95 percent of scientists believe this is happening with 100 percent confidence temperatures are rising.

Michio Kaku

And I think it's because good cons are all based on the victim's need, and the successful con artist is the one, I guess, who can exploit that. I remember reading something about this, that one of the great traits of confidence tricksters is the level that they flatter their victim.

Alfred Molina

Making films is about having absolute and foolish confidence; the challenge for all of us is to have the heart of a poet and the skin of an elephant.

Mira Nair

I have confidence that we can form this kind of national community.

Barbara Jordan

You're always going to survive the pain of loss. I can live with that confidence inside of me.

Hope Solo

Art helped give me confidence.

Jeff Koons

When I wasn't as attractive as I am now, I suffered at the hands of cruel children and their taunts until I realised that confidence and a bit of aesthetic care can overcome that.

Johnny Vegas

I am concerned about any attrition in customer traffic at Starbucks, but I don't want to use the economy, commodity prices or consumer confidence as an excuse.

Howard Schultz

I didn't have any confidence in my beauty when I was young. I felt like a character actress, and I still do.

Meryl Streep

I certainly direct with confidence even if I'm not confident. I learned early on as an actor that confidence can be faked, and it's not always a terrible thing to do. A lot of times if people feel you're confident, then they're confident.

George Clooney

Trust is a core currency of any relationship. Sometimes our need to control and micromanage everything erodes our confidence in ourselves and others. The truth: People are much more capable than we think. A hearty dose of trust is often what's needed to unlock the magic. Go ahead, have faith.

Kris Carr

I believe that my clothes can give people a better image of themselves - that it can increase their feelings of confidence and happiness.

Giorgio Armani

Now, honestly, every movie set that I go on, I walk onto set with the confidence that there is nothing that they can throw at me that's gonna surprise me.

Emma Watson

I have no control over what people think of me but I have 100% control of what I think of myself, and that is so important. And not just about your body, but so many ways of confidence. You're constantly learning how to be confident, aren't you?

Beth Ditto

Big government inevitably drives an upward distribution of wealth to those whose wealth, confidence and sophistication enable them to manipulate government.

George Will

Being successful at a very young age gave me the confidence and the capability to try out other things.

Joshua Lederberg

I think it was always there and it was maybe a matter of bringing it out. It was harder than I thought it would be and I had to try harder. I had to regain my confidence, maybe the most important thing. I have learned a lot to relax. I know what I can do now, and I do it.

Guy Lafleur

If you tell your own story to your children - that includes your positive moments and your negative moments, and how you overcame them - you give your children the skills and the confidence they need to feel like they can overcome some hardship that they've felt.

Bruce Feiler

I fall asleep feeling beautiful. Then, in the morning, before I leave the house, I say five things I love about myself, like 'You have really pretty eyes.' That way I can go out into the world with that little bit of extra confidence. It's a feel-good protein shake in my back pocket in case someone messes with me that day.

Jennifer Love Hewitt

A lot of men do have a fear of my ultra-femininity. Sometimes people say I look like a drag queen, that I look scary, but I think that's a fear of my confidence. Most women in contemporary culture pare down their femininity, so there's a slight androgyny about them, and I think men have got used to seeing that.

Paloma Faith

It's important to have people around you with enough confidence to say if you are not acting in a good way. Normally, when you are at the top, people say everything is fantastic. Probably in that moment it is what you want to hear, but it's best to be reminded how to act properly.

Rafael Nadal

I have written some songs, but I would really call what I've done poetry at the end of the day, because I'll sit with my guitar for hours and hours on end for, like, a week and then I won't touch it for a month. I also just have no confidence. And you know what? I don't have time, because I'd rather be doing other things, like knitting.

Amanda Seyfried

We are all afraid for our confidence, for the future, for the world. That is the nature of the human imagination. Yet every man, every civilization, has gone forward because of its engagement with what it has set itself to do.

Jacob Bronowski

In my view, it's irreverence, foolish confidence and naivety combined with persistence, open mindedness and a continual ability to learn that created Facebook, Google, Yahoo, eBay, Microsoft, Apple, Juniper, AOL, Sun

Microsystems and others.

Vinod Khosla

With such thoughts in your mind, now that you have resolved to love Him and please Him with all your strength, your only fear should be to fear God too much and to place too little confidence in Him.

Alphonsus Liguori

I've said this before, but I believe more than ever that confidence is sexier than any body part.

Aimee Mullins

It is also a good rule not to put overmuch confidence in the observational results that are put forward until they are confirmed by theory.

Arthur Eddington

Obama promised a return to competence and confidence and asked the nation to believe again that the government could do big things well. In the end, he got his big thing, a once-in-a-generation revision to the basic social compact, a commitment of health coverage to nearly all Americans. He has yet to prove he can do it well.

Nancy Gibbs

What I think I sell with my clothes is confidence, so hopefully all my dresses, my accessories, are friends to the women. When you open the closet, and your eyes are swollen, and you don't like the way you look, you go to your friends.

Diane von Furstenberg

Just be confident. I think confidence is the most attractive part of a person.

Curtis Jackson

It was helpful to have the confidence of youth that came from a lack of desperation. I thought, 'If I don't succeed, I'll go back to school and study.'

Olivia Wilde

I'm no diva but I can be annoying in a recording studio. Of course I try to be a diva in terms of confidence of performance and owning a song but I've never behaved like one in terms of the negative connotations of the word.

Nicole Scherzinger

For most entertainers, there is a single experience, one defining moment, when confidence replaces the self-doubt that most of us wrestle with.

Charley Pride

I think children learning to cook can be such a wonderful thing. It can help build confidence, make them feel good about themselves. It helped me build my ego and even start to get acceptance at school. I'd bring things to class that I'd cooked at home.

Giada De Laurentiis

I feel confidence in myself, but at the same time there's these cracks in the facade and those little things underneath that are unstable.

Pete Wentz

Confidence is one of the sexiest things.

Katherine Jenkins

Without boxing, because of my neighborhoods, who knows what would have happened to me. It was always about following the leader. And I definitely was not a leader. Boxing gave me discipline; a sense of self. It made me more outspoken. It gave me more confidence.

Sugar Ray Leonard

You know, when Michael Jackson does the moonwalk, he's showing off! When Prince or Hendrix do a guitar solo, it's confidence! I would hate to be at a show and some nervous wreck is sweating up there and doesn't feel like he deserves to be there.

Bruno Mars

When you really believe in God, it gives you a courage, a confidence that enables you to meet the things coming.

Della Reese

I think there have always been funny women, from Carol Burnett to Joan Rivers. When the audience sees a woman, they innately know she's worked twice as hard to get there, she's had to prove that she can be the leader, first, and then be funny on top of it. She has to emit a confidence that she's in control.

Wendy Liebman

I had so much fun developing and launching my first fragrance with Avon, so for my second fragrance, I really wanted to add a little more edge. Outspoken Intense is a provocative blend of sexy confidence and daring femininity that captures the thrill and excitement of being centre stage.

Fergie

We need to have a pro-growth policy put in place that offers people hope and offers the opportunity for businesses to expand and for them to have confidence in what the world is going to look like for the next two or three or four years with respect to economic policy.

Dick Cheney

The notion of a universality of human experience is a confidence trick and the notion of a universality of female experience is a clever confidence trick.

Angela Carter

Certain it is that a great responsibility rests upon the statesmen of all nations, not only to fulfill the promises for reduction in armaments, but to maintain the confidence of the people of the world in the hope of an enduring peace.

Frank B. Kellogg

Recovery measures work better when they raise confidence - as Franklin D. Roosevelt understood. His fireside chats, and his inaugural address proclaiming he would fight the Great Depression with the same resolve he would muster against a foreign foe, were aimed at reassuring Americans.

Christina Romer

Superstition is only the fear of belief, while religion is the confidence.

Marguerite Gardiner

Acquire the habit of speaking to God as if you were alone with Him, familiarly and with confidence and love, as to the dearest and most loving of friends.

Alphonsus Liguori

You are affected by the surroundings, the mood of people, by confidence. I am no different.

Michael Owen

I feel comfortable in Spanish, I chat like a parrot, but I don't have the confidence in Spanish that I do in English.

Sandra Cisneros

Each day, you get an ounce more confidence. When we're playing like we are, there's no reason not to.

Drew Brees

Success gave me confidence as an artist. And now I'm able to do what I want without anybody thinking it's dumb.

Amy Lee

It goes without saying that the desire to accomplish the task with more confidence, to avoid wasting time and labour, and to spare our experimental animals as much as possible, made us strictly observe all the precautions taken by surgeons in respect to their patients.

Ivan Pavlov

Confidence is contagious, but so is failure. Even the Yankees will lose if you persuade them that they will.

Rosabeth Moss Kanter

The more we refuse to buy into our inner critics - and our external ones too - the easier it will get to have confidence in our choices, and to feel comfortable with who we are - as women and as mothers.

Arianna Huffington

With each year that's gone by, and as I grow up and get older, I've become more mature, of course, but you have a sense of who you are, and you find confidence in that.

Hope Solo

I think I'm learning to be bolder in my career choices and be more confident in my personal life. I haven't always felt very secure as an individual, but now I feel I certain confidence and sense of self that gets me through the day a lot better than before.

Winona Ryder

It's not a field, I think, for people who need to have success every day: if you can't live with a nightly sort of disaster, you should get out. I wouldn't describe myself as lacking in confidence, but I would just say that the ghosts you chase you never catch.

Michael Korda

One of Obama's most impressive attributes is his quiet confidence: Voters sense that he is comfortable in his own skin, a dedicated father and friend who won't waste time with the phony rituals of Washington.

Ron Fournier

I always try to set a positive example for my generation and promote confidence.

Keke Palmer

Confidence in golf means being able to concentrate on the problem at hand with no outside interference.

Tom Watson

I missed so many opportunities along the way to do what I wanted to do because I didn't have the confidence to tell myself, much less anybody else, 'Yes, this is the business I wanted to be a part of, and not feeling that I had the talent... and letting it go all the way through Notre Dame and then through two years of Navy service.

Regis Philbin

My day jobs... I knew I was bad at those, so I didn't really have the confidence to think that I could do comedy. But I knew I hated the day jobs.

Dave Attell

The point about hope is that it is something that occurs in very dark moments. It is like a flame in the darkness; it isn't like a confidence and a promise.

John Berger

My parents weren't extremely successful financially, but they were happy people. They gave me confidence.

Jack Wagner

A sportswriter's life means never sitting with your wife or family at the games. Still working after everyone has gone to the party... Digging beneath a coach's lies, not to forget those of athletic directors and general managers and owners of pro teams. Keeping a confidence. Risking it.

Dan Jenkins

The team should have implicit confidence in the captain's decisions.

Lord Mountbatten

P.E. was my life in school. Without it, I wouldn't be standing here. It gave me confidence when I was an overweight kid with a speech impediment.

Herschel Walker

With silly stuff, it's seventy-five percent confidence. I always tell people that it's because I'm nervous about getting that next laugh and I need to hear it. I always want to condense a joke.

Tim Vine

In the morning, before I leave the house, I say five things I love about myself, like 'You have really pretty eyes.' That way I can go out into the world with that little bit of extra confidence.

Jennifer Love Hewitt

Feminism was for women, and men never had an equivalent movement or discourse in its wake, so of course the sons of men who witnessed the sexual revolution and feminism alike have sons who are meek and scared and feckless and twee. They don't have the confidence that comes along with instructions - even the confidence of somebody who defies them.

Julie Klausner

I gained a lot of confidence after 'IP Man' as being a true actor. I went on to tackle what it is an actor is supposed to do before a film. Do a lot of research, get into the character. That's what I did with 'Dragon.'

Donnie Yen

France and Italy have not yet signed this treaty or agreed to naval limitation as between those nations, but I have confidence that in time they will do so.

Frank B. Kellogg

Coaches can teach you two things: confidence and technique.

Didier Drogba

I've always had confidence. Before I was famous, that confidence got me into trouble. After I got famous, it just got me into more trouble.

Bruce Willis

When Kate was born, she was born into a world of joy and happiness and confidence. The difference between the children is night and day. She's happy, she's thriving, she's full of self-confidence. I tell her she's beautiful every day before I send her off to school.

Lynn Johnston

The first internal relation that is essential to a secret society is the reciprocal confidence of its members.

Georg Simmel

There's a certain confidence that comes with being sure about the way the world works.

John Legend

I think the most attractive thing for me when I meet a guy is confidence and him being comfortable in his own skin. I like someone who doesn't need approval or validation.

Minka Kelly

When public access to voting is impaired or when public confidence in voting is diluted, democracy suffers and our freedom is less secure.

DeForest Soaries

An artist, under pain of oblivion, must have confidence in himself, and listen only to his real master: Nature.

Auguste Renoir

My goal is to give young girls confidence in this world so they can be more like men in the decision-making process.

Jackee Harry

When you give a team life, give a team confidence, anything can happen in a Game 7.

Paul Pierce

Sexiness is about confidence and individuality. I can't keep my eyes off the women you see in cities like London, New York and Paris - the way they carry themselves and put themselves together are always so unique.

Christina Hendricks

For years, I always thought it was hilarious that I was this fitness guru, because fitness was just a tool I utilized to help people improve their confidence. For me, it's never been about fitness. It's always been about helping to empower people.

Jillian Michaels

You learn so much from competition you gain confidence every time you have to step up and perform.

Natalie Gulbis

My confidence wavers between being genuine and being insecure.

Bob Saget

Experience tells you what to do; confidence allows you to do it.

Stan Smith

I view my pitching on how confident I was out there, period. And if I lose that confidence, I can become a prisoner of my own mind.

Barry Zito

I have total confidence in Beaute Prestige International to accompany me in creating a perfume that interprets my work and my world.

Azzedine Alaia

You have to figure out what's important and keep the main points, though I will swing a little outside the box. It affords me the freedom to find out who the character is, and it's been a positive technique for me. I'm not saying everyone should change words, but if you can do it with confidence, you may nail it.

Dawn Olivieri

Growing up, I started developing confidence in what I felt. My parents helped me to believe in myself. I wasn't the best looking guy, I wasn't the best athlete in the world, but they made me feel good about myself.

Herschel Walker

The belief may be too often mistaken, but the illusion of coming into direct contact with the past is intoxicating and persuasive, and can result in an interpretation that carries conviction. Sometimes confidence is all that's needed.

Charles Rosen

I think I have a degree of confidence, but I also have terrible insecurity, like anybody does.

Ben Whishaw

I don't lack confidence. I don't sweat. I don't want to get too

Zen on you, but I have to run my own race.

Brad Grey

I used to say in the cabinet room, 'confidence is not like a can of Popeye spinach - you can't take the top off and swallow it down.' You know, confidence has to be earned.

Paul Keating

Hollywood is a suction for your confidence or your faith or your togetherness. Just walking on the street you can feel it.

Robin Wright

Clothes can transform your mood and confidence.

Alice Temperley

To restore and keep the public's confidence in the integrity of their government, state government and its officials must be open, honest and transparent.

John Lynch

'Aqualung' marks the point at which I had the confidence as a songwriter and as a guitar player to actually pick up and play the guitar and be at the forefront of the band. It's also the album on which I began to address religious issues in my music, and I think that happened simply because the time was right for it.

Ian Anderson

A business of high principle generates greater drive and effectiveness because people know that they can do the right thing decisively and with confidence.

Marvin Bower

The ultimate ground of faith and knowledge is confidence in God.

Charles Hodge

By the time I left college, I had won every award you could win - I was Mr. Man! Then I got drafted by the Giants, and you step in that locker room, and you feel inferior in every way. You just have to stick around long enough to give yourself the opportunity to build your confidence.

Michael Strahan

A confidence problem exists on the part of the people of the region who desire democratic rule in principle, but remain suspicious of both the fashion with which democratization is presented and the purposes of the democratic world.

Recep Tayyip Erdogan

Confidence and a good sense of humor can usually win a chick over.

Danny McBride

My first impression when I made it through was 'Good, because I'm going to prove to you that I deserve to be here', because they told me that sometimes I lack confidence in my performance and sometimes I'm not as consistent as they'd like me to be.

Naima Adedapo

When there's ever a breakthrough, a true breakthrough, you can go back and find a time period when the consensus was 'well, that's nonsense!' so what that means is that a true creative researcher has to have confidence in nonsense.

Burt Rutan

The big gap between the ability of actors is confidence.

Kathleen Turner

I think what is happening is I think first of all there is confidence in the U.K. economy. We're in a German rather than a Greek position in international financial markets, which is very positive and keeps our debt service costs down, and we're also beginning to see real evidence of rebalancing.

Vince Cable

Not only is there no need of an intermediary through whom He would want you to speak to Him, but He finds His delight in having you treat with Him personally and in all confidence.

Alphonsus Liguori

When I receive letters from girls that say, 'You give me confidence,' I think, 'Wow, this is amazing.' That's my goal: to let people know it's truly what's on the inside that counts.

Amber Riley

I was desperately shy when I was wee. Totally lacked confidence socially. When I look back at school photographs, I'm always the one shrinking in the back. What I really wanted to do was become a writer, and I don't think the residue of that has ever gone away. I still feel the ultimate achievement would be to write a novel.

Anne-Marie Duff

There is a degree of confidence exhibited towards strangers in Sweden, especially in hotels, at post-stations, and on board the inland steamers, which tells well for the general honesty of the people.

Bayard Taylor

Even when I'm playing someone named 'Fat Amy.' I'm all about confidence and attitude.

Rebel Wilson

I was feeling a lot of confidence, so I wanted to take advantage of that and keep playing.

Gabriela Sabatini

There's a tendency in politics to attribute bad motivation much too quickly, and the sooner you attribute bad motivation to someone you disagree with, the harder it is to find some common ground to make some progress that would give people confidence that you got it more right than wrong.

Peter Welch

Golf is a matter of confidence. If you think you cannot do it, there is no chance you will.

Henry Cotton

Even if I were knocked down by one gunshot it wouldn't affect our democracy and I wasn't knocked down and I have great confidence in our democracy and in Taiwan and in the people of Taiwan.

Chen Shui-bian

Always the eternal optimist, President Reagan instilled confidence and optimism at a time both were in short supply in our country.

Jim Ramstad

When you don't win games, yeah, you lose confidence. That's normal.

Didier Drogba

It's just kind of empowering when you become a mother. You just get overwhelmed with this new confidence and you feel really in control of your life. It's been beautiful.

Nelly Furtado

American actors are all muscular, tanned, white teeth and they have this indestructible confidence. We British are all... Dare I say it? Pessimistic.

Max Irons

I once saw an elaborate landscape in a gallery, drawn in pencil, that took my breath away. Then I realized the artist probably didn't have enough confidence to use a pen.

Garry Shandling

I think that glamour is about confidence and really owning the look.

Monique Lhuillier

The cologne you pick should make you feel good when you go out with it. I think confidence comes across more than any other of our attributes.

Mark Ronson

Coming from bad results, you have more tension and you get more into the game, maybe. You never know which is best. I prefer to come from good results. You have more confidence and you believe you are doing things well. But in football everything can change very quickly.

Tito Vilanova

Democratic elections alone do not remedy the crisis of confidence in government. Moreover, there is no viable justification for a democratic system in which public participation is limited to voting.

Beth Simone Noveck

Our feeling is that the most important thing on a set is that actors have enough confidence to try different things. If there's stress or tension, they won't go out on a limb because they won't want to embarrass themselves if they don't feel completely comfortable.

Peter Farrelly

Some of the greatest actors on the planet are the most insecure people. Now I don't know if that insecurity necessarily equates to a lack of confidence. Some people are just very shy individuals. You give them a character to play and a script, and you put them in front of a camera or on a stage, and they just go.

Eric Dane

Confidence is king in golf.

Jason Dufner

I lost my confidence.

Pat Summitt

I think that's what helped us: confidence, respect, the desire to work hard.

Ed O'Brien

But I guess the lesson is this: If you don't have confidence in yourself and think that you are worth hiring, or whatever it is, you can't expect anyone else to.

Sam Donaldson

We found on our journey, as well as in the place where we stopped, that they treated us with as much confidence and good-will as if they had known us all their lives.

Junipero Serra

When you have confidence, you can do anything.

Sloane Stephens

We've played with a lot of confidence and that's been the key so far. Hopefully, we can take more confidence into the playoffs.

Teemu Selanne

I've always been blessed with confidence. I am a glass-half-full person. My first movie, 'Private Benjamin,' got turned down by every studio until the very last one, but I just kept thinking, 'Why are you people not seeing that this is a hit movie? What is wrong with you?'

Nancy Meyers

One of the things that we can say with confidence is that we will have much lighter, much stronger materials, and this will reduce the cost of air flight, and the cost of rockets.

Ralph Merkle

I have two bowls of confidence for breakfast each morning.

Eric Bristow

It's all about confidence and how you feel about yourself. There's no such thing as a perfect woman. I like imperfections - that's what makes you unique.

Hayley Hasselhoff

I can tell women's confidence levels rise when they wear

heels.

Eric Mabius

Sharpe is my favorite role of all that I've played. He's a
very complex character. He knows that he's a good soldier,
but he will always have to fight the prejudice of aristocratic
officers because of his rough working-class upbringing. On
the battlefield, he's full of confidence - but off it, he is
unsure, a bit shy and ill at ease.

Sean Bean

I don't speak English, so I'll just have to win the trust and
confidence of the fans with my performance on the field.

Masahiro Tanaka

I wouldn't be where I am, if not for Jamaica. My formative
years were here. I wouldn't have the confidence that I have
if I wasn't born here, because growing up here I knew I
could become anybody I wanted to become. There was no
ceiling on top of me.

Michael Lee-Chin

No matter where you are, the root of you is designed from a young age. So if my confidence was taken as a child, you can gain back a lot of the confidence, but that root of the cavity will still be there.

Russell Peters

I'm a combination between extreme insecurity and extreme confidence.

Alexandra Daddario

As a scouting department, with the confidence we have in our player development, if a guy has the potential that we think they have and the makeup and they stay healthy, we think they will be a productive Major Leaguer. We take a lot of pride in that.

Roy Clark

I feel so gratified about having finished college. I learned how to articulate myself. It gave me confidence more than anything. And also the ability to analyze the text.

Maggie Gyllenhaal

Believing in yourself and what you do is so important. It took me a long time to find that confidence. If you're an artist and you're taking risks, then you're doing something right if some people don't get it.

Kate Voegele

I am here before you tonight to dedicate this administration to bringing a new renaissance of neighborhood life and community spirit, a renewal of confidence in the future of our city and a revival of opportunity for all Chicago.

Jane Byrne

If you ask me why I've succeeded, it's because I was in the Royal Marines. You have this unbelievable sense of achievement and of overcoming adversity. That's the confidence it breeds.

Brian McDermott

You always have these moments when projects are over when you wonder if you'll ever work again. In the end, what it comes down to is that it's a fine line between becoming too enamored of your own success and maintaining the confidence to do what you do and do it well. That's the line every actor, if they're lucky, has to walk.

Justin Kirk

Affliction is a school of virtue; it corrects levity, and interrupts the confidence of sinning.

Francis Atterbury

The American woman is more stylish than any other in the world. She understands the power of good style and has the confidence to feel comfortable.

Max Azria

Even institutions of State, such as the judiciary, were seriously weakened, to the extent that the citizenry justifiably feared a breakdown in law and order. The business community was hit by a slump in sales and confidence, leading to reduced earnings and loss of jobs.

Kamisese Mara

Finishing overall champion at the World Series in both the individual and synchro events has given me great confidence and I'm pleased I've been diving with consistency.

Tom Daley

I feel like more than 80% of the world wouldn't get up in front of 40 million people and dance on national television, and if I have the confidence to do that then that's a step ahead in my life for me in terms of personal goals. I will gain a lot of confidence on all aspects right there.

Rob Kardashian

If wearing the Spanx helps you get looks, and you feel that energy and response, and you're rocking your body with confidence, that's still how you'll feel about yourself when you get home and take the Spanx off... If your attitude improves from the Spanx, wear the Spanx!

Lisa Ann Walter

Here in Australia we do get impacted by global economic events. But we should have some confidence that our economy has got strong underlying fundamentals.

Julia Gillard

Charlize Theron is perfect. She holds herself with so much poise and grace. I don't know if she looks so good because she has the best body or because she has the confidence to feel comfortable in what she's wearing.

Alexandra Daddario

I think to take your shirt off, you need to have a great body and more than that, confidence and attitude. It's all related. A great body equals confidence, and confidence equals attitude. And when you put all three together, you get a Salman Khan! And that's not me.

Riteish Deshmukh

I think, head up and shoulders back. Not only does it make you look taller and thinner but it gives you confidence and boosts your self-esteem.

Shelley Long

As an actor, when you are called upon to do a job, you are oftentimes convinced you can't do it. You say to yourself 'I don't have the talent for this; they are going to figure out I'm a fraud.' And then you watch how the others do it, and fake your confidence.

Erich Bergen

My colleagues have expressed confidence in my ability to articulate our conservative message and to provide new focus to our efforts in the General Assembly.

Philip E. Berger

And so we try to address those concerns in every way possible, recognizing, again, in the final analysis, everybody on that flight wants to be assured with the highest level of confidence that everybody else on that flight has been properly screened, and including me and you and everybody.

John Pistole

Confidence has a lot to do with interviewing - that, and timing.

Michael Parkinson

The collapse of Enron was devastating to tens of thousands of people and shook the public's confidence in corporate America.

Robert Mueller

In government institutions and in teaching, you need to inspire confidence. To achieve credibility, you have to very clearly explain what you are doing and why. The same principles apply to businesses.

Janet Yellen

I am definitely not into the exposed look. I am not one of those people who flashes their stomach or anything like that, because I don't have the confidence.

Georgie Henley

Skill and confidence are an unconquered army.

George Herbert

Public confidence in the integrity of the Government is indispensable to faith in democracy; and when we lose faith in the system, we have lost faith in everything we fight and spend for.

Adlai E. Stevenson

I think that feeling that if one believed absolutely in any cause, then one must have the confidence, the self-certainty, to go through with that particular course of action.

Wole Soyinka

I have a confidence about my life that comes from standing tall on my own two feet.

Jane Fonda

I used to not be confident. My father certainly didn't add to my confidence. When I was 17 or 18, I was voted the most beautiful girl in England by the association of press photographers. When they called Daddy for a comment, he said, 'I'm amazed. She's a nice looking girl, but nothing special.'

Joan Collins

My main job is to live with deep contentment, joy, and confidence in my everyday experience of life with God. Everything else is job number two.

John Ortberg

We started a movement... to build character, citizenship and confidence in young people.

Andrew Shue

I had lots of trouble in school as a child, and I lost confidence. Teachers thought I was stupid. I learned to read very late, when I was 11. Dyslexia wasn't recognized then, and the assumption was you were incapable of thinking.

Richard Rogers

Citizens, the priority now is to recover trust between the Egyptian - amongst the Egyptians and to have trust and confidence in our economy and international reputation and the fact that the change that we have embarked on will carry on and there's no going back to the old days.

Hosni Mubarak

School is very important; it was very important for me. It gave me an enormous amount of confidence, especially at Yale where we were dealing with all the classics. In dealing with the classics, you are dealing with the very best.

Enrico Colantoni

The first time I walked into the Olympic athlete village seeing the Visa ATM machine with my picture on it and the Chinese characters saying 'Destiny.' For some reason, it just boosted my confidence and it was before I had even worked out or had my first training or competed.

Nastia Liukin

I have confidence in my personality, because I think that if I talk to people hopefully they will like me, but I don't have confidence in my body.

Georgie Henley

Disarmament, with mutual honor and confidence, is a continuing imperative.

Dwight D. Eisenhower

To me, getting muscular was the first thing I ever achieved by working at it, and it was a game changer for me, because it was the first time I ever had confidence.

Henry Rollins

The confidence in another man's virtue is no light evidence

of a man's own, and God willingly favors such a confidence.

Michel de Montaigne

Union of religious sentiments begets a surprising confidence.

James Madison

The American people I talk to don't spend every moment thinking, 'How can I tax my neighbor more than they're being taxed?' They say, 'How can I get a good job? How can my kids get good jobs? How can seniors have a confidence in their future when they know that Social Security, Medicare and Medicaid are bankrupt?'

Mitt Romney

When I was younger, I really struggled with confidence.

Jurnee Smollett

I always thought that I was an important musician. If you don't have that confidence, why would you go on and do it?

Yoko Ono

I wouldn't describe myself as lacking in confidence, but I would just say that - the ghosts you chase you never catch.

John Malkovich

Danger breeds best on too much confidence.

Pierre Corneille

Confidence and superiority: It's the usual fundamentalist stuff: I've got the truth, and you haven't.

Jeanette Winterson

Faith is the confidence, the assurance, the enforcing truth, the knowing.

Robert Collier

I think that if my kids are completely convinced of God's unfailing love for them, whether they fail or not, they'll have confidence to persevere in life.

Amy Grant

I think that many things that go on in an art school have a tendency to undermine confidence, and that shouldn't be part of the ballgame, ever.

Lewis Black

Boys and girls, have confidence in the direction and counsel and advice of your parents and grandparents who love you more than anybody else in the world does.

James E. Faust

When Hollywood sees a good story about a man who sells confidence, they see themselves and they like it.

Ben Stein

Confidence is one of the sexiest things in guys and girls.

Danica McKellar

With any kind of artistic thing, it's a muscle, like any athlete, and the moment you're not doing it, you lose all confidence. That's why I'm terrible with down time.

Daniel Radcliffe

Every writer knows that unless you were born gifted with either supreme confidence or outsize ego, handing in your work holds, in some cases, admitted terror. If that's too strong, at least fairly high anxiety.

Dick Cavett

I believe you have constructive accidents en route through a novel only because you have mapped a clear way. If you have confidence that you have a clear direction to take, you always have confidence to explore other ways; if they prove to be mere digressions, you'll recognize that and make the necessary revisions.

John Irving

I want to try doing sportier things, kite surfing and paddle surfing - I think it would give me that extra confidence.

Vanessa Hudgens

I suggest that going to Mars means permanence on the planet - a mission by which we are building up a confidence level to become a two-planet species.

Buzz Aldrin

I want girls to feel the confidence you get from being smart. They get so many messages that tell them the most important thing is to be beautiful.

Danica McKellar

When I'm out on the football field, I have so much confidence in what I'm doing.

Tom Brady

I've always had a process that I do before I even get to set or go to the location. I work privately, and it almost feels like therapy between me and who I'm playing. So I have this inner life that's there and it gives me a confidence, too, that when I'm playing the role I know every question.

Kirsten Dunst

I sometimes lack confidence in public, although I am proud enough inwardly.

Robert Schumann

Bad food is made without pride, by cooks who have no pride, and no love. Bad food is made by chefs who are indifferent, or who are trying to be everything to everybody, who are trying to please everyone... Bad food is fake food... food that shows fear and lack of confidence in people's ability to discern or to make decisions about their lives.

Anthony Bourdain

Dream small dreams. If you make them too big, you get overwhelmed and you don't do anything. If you make small goals and accomplish them, it gives you the confidence to go on to higher goals.

John H. Johnson

A lot of people, when a guy scores a lot of goals, think, 'He's a great player', because a goal is very important, but a great player is a player who can do everything on the field. He can do assists, encourage his colleagues, give them confidence to go forward. It is someone who, when a team does not do well, becomes one of the leaders.

Pele

My style has changed and evolved mainly because I've grown to have more confidence in myself.

Kevin Durant

Health is the greatest possession. Contentment is the greatest treasure. Confidence is the greatest friend. Non-being is the greatest joy.

Lao Tzu

You just have to be yourself and go full with confidence and be courageous.

Gabby Douglas

Confidence and empowerment are cousins in my opinion. Empowerment comes from within and typically it's stemmed and fostered by self-assurance. To feel empowered is to feel free and that's when people do their best work. You can't fake confidence or empowerment.

Amy Jo Martin

Crystallize your goals. Make a plan for achieving them and set yourself a deadline. Then, with supreme confidence, determination and disregard for obstacles and other people's criticisms, carry out your plan.

Paul J. Meyer

Faith is a living, daring confidence in God's grace, so sure and certain that a man could stake his life on it a thousand times.

Martin Luther

Being glamorous is about strength and confidence. It's black and white - dramatic. You have to be strong.

Catherine Zeta-Jones

Censorship reflects a society's lack of confidence in itself.

Potter Stewart

Working with great people makes you great; you learn a lot and it also gives you the experience and confidence to move on with your own career.

Nas

Honor bespeaks worth. Confidence begets trust. Service brings satisfaction. Cooperation proves the quality of leadership.

James Cash Penney

I think that the power is the principle. The principle of
moving forward, as though you have the confidence to
move forward, eventually gives you confidence when you
look back and see what you've done.

Robert Downey, Jr.

The circulation of confidence is better than the circulation
of money.

James Madison

The most important thing for me is having a relationship
with God. To know that the owner, the creator of the
universe loves you, sent His Son to die for your sins; that's
very empowering. Knowing Him and knowing that He
loves me gives me encouragement and confidence to move
forward.

Benjamin Carson

Who is a professional? A professional is someone who has

a combination of competence, confidence and belief. A water diviner is a professional. A traditional midwife is a professional. A traditional bone setter is a professional. These are professionals all over the world. You find them in any inaccessible village around the world.

Bunker Roy

In fact, the confidence of the people is worth more than money.

Carter G. Woodson

Great leaders don't need to act tough. Their confidence and humility serve to underscore their toughness.

Simon Sinek

Our government is founded upon the intelligence of the people. I for one do not despair of the republic. I have great confidence in the virtue of the great majority of the people, and I cannot fear the result.

Andrew Jackson

Working together in concert more smoothly not only helps

us move more quickly; it changes the nature of what we can undertake. When we have the confidence that we can orchestrate the group effort required to realize them, we dare bigger dreams.

Justin Rosenstein

Power without a nation's confidence is nothing.

Catherine the Great

Style is whatever you want to do, if you can do it with confidence.

George Clinton

If you have no confidence in self, you are twice defeated in the race of life. With confidence, you have won even before you have started.

Marcus Tullius Cicero

Confidence is contagious. So is lack of confidence.

Vince Lombardi

Most of my confidence came from being with ladies, because I certainly wasn't getting any acting jobs.

Vin Diesel

We should remember it wasn't so long ago that confidence in New York was in short supply.

Michael Bloomberg

My friend made me a leather dress for the MTV awards. It gives you confidence, wearing something you love.

Cat Deeley

We can't wait for Washington. Business leaders are going to have to galvanize their own constituencies and do everything they can to demonstrate confidence in the economy, and I think that can be contagious.

Howard Schultz

I think people are rapidly losing confidence in the political class, and I don't blame them.

Adnan Pachachi

After watching wrestling for 20 years, I thought I had enough confidence to do it. There were no wrestling schools at the time.

Hulk Hogan

Therefore, let us not despair, but instead, survey the position, consider carefully the action we must take, and then address ourselves to our common task in a mood of sober resolution and quiet confidence, without haste and without pause.

Arthur Henderson

The Egyptians have grown in confidence, they've tasted freedom, and there's no way back.

Mohamed ElBaradei

What I see in the corporate sector is very clearly an issue of a major shortfall in the issue of, what some people call confidence, but whatever you want to call it. Clearly people are looking out in the very distant future and they are saying that it is too complex.

Alan Greenspan

I really like guys who have confidence, but not the cocky over-the-top confidence.

Carly Rae Jepsen

To be a preacher requires two apparently contradictory qualities: confidence and humility.

Timothy Radcliffe

Getting up to Zaire - getting ready to fight Muhammad Ali - I thought this will be a matter of just a little exercise. I'll probably knock him out in three rounds. Two, three - maybe three and a half rounds. That was the most confidence I had in my whole life.

George Foreman

I've always been inspired by women, and my mission was to inspire women. I always wanted to become a certain kind of woman, and I became that woman through fashion. It was a dialogue. I would see that the wrap dress made those women confident, and made them act with confidence.

Diane von Furstenberg

What's the worst thing that can happen to a quarterback? He loses his confidence.

Terry Bradshaw

Tim also has enough confidence so that it always looks like a Tim Burton film, but it really is collaborative. You're allowed to do it your way but of course he's always going to choose his way.

Helena Bonham Carter

Strengthening our identity is one way of reinforcing people's confidence and sense of citizenship and well-being.

David Blunkett

If you wish to strengthen your confidence in God still more, often recall the loving way in which He has acted toward you, and how mercifully He has tried to bring you out of your sinful life, to break your attachment to the things of earth and draw you to His love.

Alphonsus Liguori

I have no confidence issues with the impact or the quality of the music. No one in hip-hop, before this point and to this point, with all due respect, has done this.

Mos Def

When I meet large women who walk with confidence and are articulate and really have an understanding of how they walk in this world, I love them so deeply for being able to overcome such unbelievable odds.

Camryn Manheim

My mother is an amazing woman. Not only did she manage the entire household, she noticed a gift in each of her kids and instilled confidence in all of us that that gift would take us wherever we wanted to go.

Barbara Corcoran

For so many years, I felt so insecure, so inferior, and I still have those moments, but I have a newfound confidence since I got in shape and changed my diet.

Marc Jacobs

People who ask confidently get more than those who are hesitant and uncertain. When you've figured out what you want to ask for, do it with certainty, boldness and confidence. Don't be shy or feel intimidated by the experience. You may face some unexpected criticism, but be prepared for it with confidence.

Jack Canfield

I've lived in Washington now for 44 years, and that's a lot of folly to witness up close. Whatever confidence and optimism I felt towards the central government when I got here on January 1, 1970 has pretty much dissipated at the hands of the government.

George Will

Both of my girls have very high self-esteem because they were both able to master certain things; I should think that's good for their confidence.

Amy Chua

National markets are held together by shared values and confidence in certain minimum standards. But in the new global market, people do not yet have that confidence.

Kofi Annan

A sight game is that I am hurt, but I aim to make you believe I am not even hurt, and with this confidence appearing on my face, I don't panic, otherwise your opponent will know that you are hurt. That's the whole art game in boxing.

Evander Holyfield

I think people look great in black. I love that what stands out is the person, especially. Black just conveys a kind of drama, even if it can be quiet drama. It does lend to the wearer a sense of confidence.

Andre Leon Talley

You can't teach talent. You can't put in what God left out - but you can teach confidence.

Gloria Naylor

Concentration, Confidence, Competitive urge, Capacity for enjoyment.

Arnold Palmer

I think you have to feel comfortable with your car. You have to go into turn one, every lap, with confidence. You have to be sure of yourself and your equipment.

Danica Patrick

I don't really care about clothes, but it's about wearing something that gives you social confidence.

Julian Casablancas

If you ask any great player or great quarterback, there's a certain inner confidence that you're as good as anybody. But you can't say who is the absolute best. To be considered is special in itself.

Dan Marino

Especially with music, people want confidence.

Grimes

What I worry about is that people are losing confidence, losing energy, losing enthusiasm, and there's a real opportunity to get them into work.

Boris Johnson

I have a friend who, if she has a bad hair day, it affects her whole mood because it is part of her sexuality, her confidence. I don't have that problem any more.

Cathy Freeman

My dad is like a cactus - introverted and tough. I'm a people person, like my mom, but I got my competitiveness from my dad. He came to this country from Belarus with nothing and built a real business. He's my hero for giving me that need to run a business and for having enormous confidence in me.

Gary Vaynerchuk

Innovation almost always is not successful the first time out. You try something, and it doesn't work, and it takes confidence to say we haven't failed yet... Ultimately, you become commercially successful.

Clayton Christensen

The mark of a truly civilized man is confidence in the strength and security derived from the inquiring mind.

Felix Frankfurter

Last year, when 'Black Swan,' 'True Grit' and 'King's Speech' all grossed over $100 million, it gave studios and independent financiers the confidence to make daring movies and not do the same old you-know-what.

Harvey Weinstein

Beauty is not skin-deep; it can be a means of self-affirmation, a true indicator of personality and confidence.

Aimee Mullins

I wish I had more confidence.

Seann William Scott

I obviously want to give a healthy body image to my own daughter. I think having good examples, eating properly, that's all one can do - and just be really loving around her. I've tried to give her confidence in who she is. I think she's all right in the confidence department.

Geri Halliwell

For if you train hard and responsibly your confidence surges to a maximum.

Floyd Patterson

I'm always astonished by the confidence my readers put in me.

Mary Karr

It is a great blessing to have light in our lives - a light that helps us see things as they really are, light that illuminates our understanding, light we can follow with confidence and perfect trust.

Margaret D. Nadauld

Wikileaks didn't help confidence with American administrations because of conversations made public so easily.

Abdallah II of Jordan

I think you can look at the British economy with confidence.

George Osborne

And in doing this I advise you to send to the best manors of your lands those of your household in whom you place most confidence to be present in August at the leading of the corn, and to guard it as aforesaid.

Robert Grosseteste

Since I've started fighting it has taught me a lot about self respect, self confidence and self control.

Gina Carano

I believe that the confidence of Hungary in me is not shaken by misfortune nor broken by my calumniators.

Lajos Kossuth

I have a high degree of confidence about India's growth potential in IT.

Sanjay Kumar

It gives me confidence to know that what I'm writing has a veracity of its own without me having to invent it. When I'm writing fiction, I must believe it to be true, or I can see no point in it.

Michael Morpurgo

I do freestyle jumping. Been doing since I was eight years old and can't quit. I'm addicted. I've broken many bones, but I ride with confidence. It's my thing - there's no high on earth like it. It's my hobby and I really enjoy it.

Vanilla Ice

Princess Diana was a nice dancer because she had confidence. In fact, when we danced together she started to lead, and I looked her in eye and went, 'No, you have to let me lead.' So I grabbed her around the waist and we were off to the races.

John Travolta

The Australian economy is resilient, but business and consumer confidence is fragile.

Julie Bishop

You need to have tremendous confidence in your work, even a touch of arrogance, chutzpah. Many very fine researchers lack intellectual daring. It's human nature to want to be cozy, secure. But that can be a cul de sac.

Vilayanur S. Ramachandran

It feels like the more I'm out there in the public eye, the more criticism I get. You need to have confidence - that's what it takes to walk out there and sing a song in front of a huge group of people.

Gwen Stefani

I ski every three years or so. I don't have the ingrained confidence that others do, but I'll happily toddle about a green or blue run.

Cherie Lunghi

Women are always told, 'You're not going to make it, its too difficult, you can't do that, don't enter this competition, you'll never win it,' - they need confidence in themselves and people around them to help them to get on.

Zaha Hadid

I worry about how accessible cosmetic surgery has become.

Of course, if it has genuinely helped people, and their confidence has grown as a result; who am I to form an opinion?

Erin O'Connor

I believe in my kids 100 percent. When you have confidence in them, they have confidence in themselves.

Michael Strahan

One of the ways to make sure policies are more transparent and to help restore people's confidence in politicians... is to ensure renewal at the highest level of office.

Pauline Marois

When I was growing up and somebody like Robert De Niro had a movie come out, it was a cultural event. Because he had such a confidence and a single mission that was so intimate.

Sean Penn

Along with age comes more confidence, so it kind of works out.

Leslie Mann

I understand how important hair is to a woman's self-esteem and confidence.

Cat Deeley

What's the worst thing that can happen to a quarterback? He loses his confidence.

Terry Brennan

I am now the Wimbledon champion, and I think that gives me even more confidence coming to the Olympics. And maybe in some ways, it maybe takes some pressure off the Olympics, because I already did win at Wimbledon this year.

Roger Federer

I believe that the Foreign Intelligence Surveillance Act must be reformed. We must improve the American public's confidence in, and perception of, our national security programs, by increasing transparency, strengthening oversight, and safeguarding civil liberties.

Dutch Ruppersberger

I think of novels in architectural terms. You have to enter at the gate, and this gate must be constructed in such a way that the reader has immediate confidence in the strength of the building.

Ian Mcewan

Celebrate your family's bleakest moments and how your relatives overcame them. In doing so, you will encounter darkness, but you'll give your children the confidence that they, too, shall overcome.

Bruce Feiler

I try to keep my confidence on the charts, but I'm a confident guy as well. You've got to be that way. If you don't think that you're the best, then you won't perform that way.

Robert Griffin III

I'm not in front of the camera, they are. I encourage them; I build up as much of their confidence and ego as possible. They've got to take control; I can't act it out.

Taylor Hackford

Wealth brings strength, strength confidence.

John Lothrop Motley

The greatest thing you can give a child is confidence.

Gail Porter

We would like to have every middle and high school become a place where there will be lots of examples of youth competence and confidence.

Bill Drayton

I was incredibly lucky that my first book found a large and loyal readership. It changed my life - from being a very withdrawn adult to living in Paris as a full-time writer. It has also given me enormous confidence.

Daniel Tammet

It's easy to say young people should believe in themselves, but the number one thing is recognizing that it's a journey, that you have to build confidence in yourself.

Andrew Shue

Have confidence that if you have done a little thing well, you can do a bigger thing well too.

David Storey

Before the sacred, people lose all sense of power and all confidence; they occupy a powerless and humble attitude toward it. And yet no thing is sacred of itself, but by my declaring it sacred, by my declaration, my judgment, my bending the knee; in short, by my - conscience.

Max Stirner

I think it's so important just to have confidence in your body. Everyone knows that confidence is sexy, and it's knowing your assets, your strengths, and just playing those up.

Marisa Miller

We have to keep the momentum going in the economy. And we have to make sure that we give small businesses as much cash and liquidity as possible so they have the confidence to hire that next worker.

Karen Mills

I find myself going out on the road to get my confidence back, because I lose it at home.

Lionel Richie

We live in a time of conflict - external and internal - when we sometimes concentrate too much on what divides us. Today, fly the Stars and Stripes with pride and confidence that what unites is far stronger.

Charlie Dent

You would have to say his number one accomplishment has been to inspire a sense of confidence in the country. That confidence, that optimism, not only gives President Obama a political cushion, but it could have a real world economic impact.

George Stephanopoulos

For me, it is very important to believe in the kind of movies

I do. 'Rang De Basanti' made me feel good about Indian cinema. The movie instilled in me a confidence so strong, that I wanted to be a part of the revolution in Bollywood.

Vir Das

When you have confidence, that's what becomes attractive to other people and makes them want to work with you and spend time with you.

Emmanuelle Chriqui

Getting out of bed in the morning is an act of false confidence.

Jules Feiffer

At some point he seemed to lose all confidence trying to break down the Berlin Wall. He was still fighting as only Kasparov can, but I could see it in his eyes that he knew he wasn't going to win one of these games.

Vladimir Kramnik

We go there with confidence, but we know there is a very fine line between success and failure in this game.

Alan Shearer

When a child grows up without a father, there is an empty place where someone must stand, providing an example of character and confidence.

Steve Largent

I always had a lot of confidence in my work and the unique flavor I like to bring to my characters, but you know I'm not a huge dreamer.

Nick Offerman

Our society has lost confidence in the power of reason, except perhaps scientific reason.

Timothy Radcliffe

I have full confidence in the IMF. It is a very strong international institution.

Jose Manuel Barroso

If you have confidence you have patience. Confidence, that

is everything.

Ilie Nastase

To win a major tournament you have to face the top teams at some point, but if you avoid those at the beginning then you can win games and build confidence. I think the key is just to get off to a good start.

Jermain Defoe

I've been training super hard at the Lopez Taekwondo Academy in Houston, which belongs to my brother Jean. For me, I think confidence is the biggest thing; it's all mental. I train with the best of the best, including my brother Steven, a five-time world champion who won Olympic gold medals.

Diana Lopez

Before the sacred, people lost all sense of power and all confidence; they occupy a powerless and humble attitude toward it. And yet no thing is sacred of itself, but by declaring it sacred, by my declaration, my judgment, my bending the knee; in short, by my - conscience.

Max Stirner

I never had the chutzpah to just come to L.A. and make it. I didn't have that confidence. I'm always surprised when I get a job.

Isla Fisher

Of any guitarist, Jimmy Page was my biggest influence. I wanted to look, think and play like him. Zeppelin had a heavy influence on Rush during our early days. Page's loose style of playing showed an immense confidence, and there are no rules to his playing.

Alex Lifeson

I've been shocked by film actors - 25 and under - having such confidence and cockiness to rewrite a scene. My background is more about the director being in control. It's all about yielding. It's an oddly submissive relationship in which you're moulded, Pygmalion-style.

Anne-Marie Duff

I do have a little bit more confidence in - or at least familiarity with - my process. For example, when it feels like it's going badly or that I'm lost, I know I'll eventually find my way because I've been through it before. But writing itself is still hard.

Sara Zarr

The idea of confidence, of the emotions of the population, is an incredibly important one in economics. John Maynard Keynes called it 'animal spirit.' And if people are feeling generally good about the future, they're more likely to spend money, to start new companies; companies are more likely to hire people, make investments.

Adam Davidson

I always thought I could play pro ball. I had confidence in my ability, You have to. If you don't who will?

Johnny Unitas

I never had any question that my parents loved me. I had a real sense of self confidence.

Jeannette Walls

I want to wake up every day and feel that I'm training harder than my competitors, that I'm dieting harder, that I'm recovering better. That's what gives me confidence when

I'm lining up on the blocks. I've never gone out to prove people wrong. I just want to be the best that I can possibly be.

Oscar Pistorius

People wrote me off, but I believed in myself. I got the confidence back, and it grew and grew. I won my first major and my last at the place that changed my life.

Pete Sampras

I basically try to visualize the team doing good things on the court the night before the game. I get shots up. There's not actually a pregame ritual that I do. I'm still trying to figure that out. I say a prayer. I go out with confidence.

Trey Burke

Everyone has attitude, and I think everyone should have attitude. But I know I have attitude, but that's just, I think if you don't have attitude, it comes only with self confidence. So if you don't have self confidence, you won't have attitude, and I think there's a difference when you have attitude and when you have arrogance.

Sania Mirza

Sports nurtures dreams of achieving self confidence and masculine striving for the skinny kid watching a boxer dance around the ring with sublime ease.

Armstrong Williams

Maybe it has something to do with turning 30. I don't feel as shy or nervous or self-conscious. I have more confidence that I can handle what life brings me. I don't feel scared to have an idea and express it.

Michelle Williams

The funny thing is I'm actually really insecure. I have a lot of girl issues - 'I'm not pretty enough,' 'I'm not skinny enough' - but there is a confidence I have in what I can do. I did tend to overcompensate to cover up other insecurities that I have.

Lindsay Pearce

There are people that have that confidence, who march into VIP areas. I assume I won't get in. I don't say, 'Do you know who I am?', but sometimes I'm with someone who says it for you. Then, I pretend to be all, 'Oh, please don't shame me!'.

Chris Lowe

Find what makes you feel comfortable. The confidence you wear your clothes in is what's really going to shine.

Hayley Hasselhoff

I think a show can work anywhere if it's done honestly, with integrity, and with confidence.

Joey McIntyre

We must regain the confidence and drive to decide our own destiny.

Roh Moo-hyun

I used to wake up and look at our analytics and think, 'What if yesterday was the last day anyone used Pinterest?' Like, everyone collectively decided, 'We're done!' Over time I got more confidence.

Ben Silbermann

Frankly speaking, it's only the script that matters to me the most. If I like the script, then I just commit to myself and go ahead with it. But I also look at the commitment and confidence of the director of the film because it's him who will shape the film.

Vidya Balan

Confidence is highly overrated when it comes to creating literature. A writer who is overly confident will not engage in the struggle to get it exactly right on the page - but rather, will assume that she's getting it right without the struggle.

Dani Shapiro

I didn't have the confidence to leave the band because of a solo career, or anything like that. I just wanted to grow.

Dee Dee Ramone

It is so often true that whether a person carries with him an atmosphere of gloom and depression or one of confidence and courage depends on his individual outlook.

James Keller

Put your faith in God and confidence in yourself.

Alberta Hunter

I'm getting more and more comfortable out on the golf course with the changes I've been making. It's really just a confidence thing in that I love being in contention.

Paula Creamer

I hope you will respond to the crisis of confidence that Watergate has created by opening up your administration and reaching out to people in a more magnanimous spirit.

Elliot Richardson

The first record I ever listened to was Elvis Presley, and I remember thinking, 'Man this guy is cool!' The swagger he had really helped my confidence, because he really made me think that a white boy could make music like this.

Jesse McCartney

I always think I know the way a novel will go. I write maps on oversized art pads like the kind I carried around in college when I was earnest about drawing. I need to have some idea of the shape of the novel, where its headed, so that I can proceed with confidence. But the truth is my characters start doing and saying things I don't expect.

Julianna Baggott

A terrorist nuclear detonation in a western city would destroy all economic confidence.

John Bruton

I liked sports but I never really had the confidence. I was always coordinated and it came easy to me, but I didn't have the confidence to go along with the physical skill.

Bradley Cooper

When writing comedy, you have to have the confidence to believe that there is only one type of relationship in the world, and we are all having it, that all men behave in the same way and so do all women.

Steven Moffat

My friends and I have always loved the Neutrogena brand and their ability to help inspire confidence. So when I found out I was actually going to be part of the Neutrogena family, I was really excited.

Miranda Cosgrove

I believe that if corporate America expects consumer confidence to be restored, they must first be honest with us.

Bennie Thompson

The monitors indicated that it was a credible election, I think, in an overall sense, it apparently is a free and fair election, so it's a real milestone and one of the things we can take some little confidence in.

Warren Christopher

You've got to have confidence and trust in your cast. You have to have confidence and trust in your director, in your editor. It's such a team effort; I really think you have to pull yourself out of it and just trust. I think the number one thing you can do is just trust everyone around you.

Reid Scott

It is obvious that putting the Arab-Israeli dispute on a

resolution track would be an important element of overcoming the confidence problem in the region.

Recep Tayyip Erdogan

Things said to a reporter in confidence should be kept in confidence.

Dorothy Kilgallen

I have great confidence in Taiwan's democracy. I have great confidence in the universal value and in basic human rights, and I have great confidence that referenda will eventually take root and become part of our daily lives in Taiwan.

Chen Shui-bian

I have great confidence in the universal value and in basic human rights and I have great confidence that referenda will eventually take root and become part of our daily lives in Taiwan.

Chen Shui-bian

When I was as you are now, towering in the confidence of

twenty-one, little did I suspect that I should be at forty-nine, what I now am.

Sarah Orne Jewett

Get more confidence by doing things that excite and frighten you.

Jessica Williams

Women were quite terrifying until I was older. I think that's partly down to confidence.

Jimmy Carr

I'm not being evasive but I am saying I'm not a scientist and I'm not directly involved in the consultation however the science must be sound, it must be agreed and the consultation must be of a high quality or no one will have any confidence in the process.

John Anderson

I want to make sure we are presenting to the South Australian people a Government that is open and accountable. I want to make sure that we maintain public confidence in government at all levels.

Jay Weatherill

South Australia has transformed. There has been a range of changes to our economy over the past 10 years in which we have genuinely set ourselves up for the future. I think we have to start behaving like that's real and project a quiet confidence in the future of our state.

Jay Weatherill

My most profound confidence is however based upon the fact that at the head of Germany there stands a man by his entire development, his desires, and striving can only have been destined by fate to lead our people into a brighter future.

Alfred Jodl

But we can turn challenges into opportunities if we look outwards to the realities of the global economy and modernise our internal institutions in ways that will equip Europe to meet that challenge and create confidence amongst the public.

John Hutton

I had the trade minister in China sit down as we were preparing for trade negotiations. He said, 'Please don't let people in the United States lose their confidence because when you lose your confidence, the rest of the world suffers'.

Jon Huntsman, Jr.

Every astronaut flew into space for a living. But while NASA has not solved the security problems, I would not put me back into a shuttle - and no other astronaut. The confidence is shaken.

Ulrich Walter

The trust institutions have in the marketplace, the confidence customers and suppliers and workers and employees have, are very important to a business's effectiveness.

Janet Yellen

Don may yawn at the idea, which he often does, but the great thing about Don, he has confidence in me and Mike and Ed and Leslie and Steve, that we're not going go out and do stories that will put people to sleep.

Morley Safer

I had very little confidence in myself as an actress.

Maude Adams

I think they do have to get it right in Sierra Leone. There has to be something in there now to establish confidence, to stabilize the situation, and then to move to some sort of political negotiations.

Alex Morrison

I have confidence in people's basic common sense.

Dixie Lee Ray

When you're young, you say it how it is, and even your views are, like, 'This is totally the truth', 'cos you don't know any difference, so there's a real confidence in your way of thinking.

Agyness Deyn

The world is likely to view any temporary extension of the

income tax cuts for the top two percent as a prelude to a long-term or permanent extension, and that would hurt economic recovery as well by undermining confidence that we're prepared to make a commitment today to bring down our future deficits.

Timothy Geithner

Give me your trust and confidence, knowing that what I seek is for the good of Fiji, for the good of us all.

Josefa Iloilo

One reason citizens, politicians and university donors sometimes lack confidence in the social sciences is that social scientists too often miss the chance to declare victory and move on to new frontiers.

Nicholas A. Christakis

The American people want us to stop spending. And so let's just give them some certainty. Let's extend the tax - the existing tax cuts. And then let's give some more tax breaks to small businesses and large. And then maybe the American people will have some confidence.

John McCain

I'm really grateful to my parents for having the confidence in me to let me go. I was terrified I might have to slink back to the village with my tail between my legs, and treated every job as though it were my last - I still do - but fortunately, I got work and things seemed to slot into place.

Sheridan Smith

I know I have experience, having worked with the likes of legendary composers like Ilaiyaraaja. And, I've been long enough with my dear friend A. R. Rahman, and we've collaborated on several musical works. All this gives me confidence.

Sivamani

No one can duplicate the confidence that RSA offers after 20 years of cryptanalytic review.

Bruce Schneier

When I tested for Billy Budd, I had that kind of confidence that comes with the certainty that you're not going to get something. I was very rough around the edges.

Terence Stamp

On a scale of one to 10, I'd rate my body confidence as a good seven. Everyone has their hang-ups, but I see my body as a training tool and I feel good about it.

Jessica Ennis

My first album was full of ideas and attempts to go in all kinds of directions. I was young. I loved making music, but I didn't have a clear path. I also lacked in confidence.

Yael Naim

If we want to build the Iraqis' confidence about our intentions in their country, if we want to stop adding fuel to the fire of insurgency and terrorism, we must clarify our intent.

John Conyers

The 100m taught me a lot and it's given me confidence.

Yohan Blake

Like our attitude to love, truth and goodness, we seem to be confident about knowing what beauty is - certain, even dogmatic - until we think hard about the idea, whereupon all confidence flies away.

Charles Jencks

For many years I have advocated 'redesigning Parliament' in a variety of ways - elect the Senate, do away with the 'confidence convention,' permit freer voting, strengthen the role of back benchers and committees, do away with ineffectual 'take note' debates, restructure question period, and so on.

Preston Manning

Not to this extent but from day one I had an awful lot of confidence when I got started.

George Thorogood

The three traits speculators must learn to manage within themselves are confidence, fear, and aggressiveness.

Larry Williams

I did a film which was considered an independent movie with Dustin Hoffman and Andy Garcia called Confidence, and that's the type of film I was willing to take a chance on that because of the caliber of people involved with the film.

Morris Chestnut

When the Americans are behind you, they're behind you 100%, and this gives you real confidence as an architect. They expect you to lead a building project - to make the kind of big and costly decisions that, in Britain, have been handed over to project managers and cost-cutters.

David Chipperfield

Gentlemen, I fervently trust that before long the principle of arbitration may win such confidence as to justify its extension to a wider field of international differences.

Henry Campbell-Bannerman

General Petraeus is not a miracle worker. He can not be successful unless the president creates greater confidence within his own team about the decisions which the president has himself made.

Jim Talent

When people have an inner sense of confidence, they're more beautiful.

Amy Carlson

I really think that's the key, part of the spiritual renewal that America needs to have, the notion that we really can have confidence in a better tomorrow.

Carol Moseley Braun

I went to stage school with a neighbor to build confidence because I was quite shy.

Alexandra Roach

We have to have a way of dealing with this that engenders confidence, trust, gives us every chance of getting the right outcome and boosts both sustainability and economic return at the same time.

John Anderson

Leaders thrive when they feel creatively empowered, when they trust the people around them, when their confidence is swelling. Leaders make mistakes when they lose that same confidence, when they're fretting about their power base, when they're reacting instead of acting.

Bill Simmons

When I was child, I never spoke. Teacher used to write remarks on my note book. My mom sent me to a trainer. I started talking, and it gave me confidence.

Boman Irani

Confidence in a bloke would be arrogance in a woman. For years, I didn't give interviews because I was scared of people judging me or thinking I was arrogant.

Alice Lowe

This is our culture, and I don't care who the musician is, if he avoids black people, then he is scared of something. He doesn't have confidence in himself or else he doesn't believe in what he's doing.

Betty Carter

With so many contradictory renditions of the biblical text, the public has lost confidence that we can actually know what the Bible says. It is an easy step from this skepticism to an indifference about what the Bible says.

Leland Ryken

With every animal, you have to build its confidence around people because people do some crazy and stupid things.

Ian Dunbar

I didn't do plays at school, because I didn't have the confidence. At 14, I was at boarding school in Devon and I suffered from dyslexia quite badly, but they had a very good department there which specialised in it.

Joseph Mawle

We have to change economic policy: create confidence, foster investment, cut the public deficit, restructure taxation and reform the labor laws.

Mariano Rajoy

I was in Beijing a month ago working on the smoke project in collaboration with an architect there, and I was asked very directly whether it was safe to breathe in the smoke.

They did not have confidence in the museum not to use harmful smoke, and they certainly didn't have confidence that the city would protect them from harmful smoke.

Olafur Eliasson

At that time I had complete confidence in Russian policy and I believed that the Western Allies deliberately allowed Russia and Germany to fight each other to the death.

Klaus Fuchs

I absolutely refuse to accept the fact that any country in the world goes into a kind of film-making crisis. What happens is they lose confidence, they lose focus and the young film-makers of any particular generation can very easily get lost in that mix. It's happened in Italy, happened in France, happened in the U.K. during my lifetime.

David Puttnam

I don't have the confidence to be a personality.

Zoe Wanamaker

I cannot approach someone; I lack the confidence when it

comes to the guy I desire. I'm very good when it comes to matchmaking and hooking others up. But I can't help my own cause.

Kangna Ranaut

I thought we were aggressive across the board defensively, and you could just see it grow. As the game went along, you could see the confidence grow. It showed in the fourth quarter.

Bill Laimbeer

I really enjoy myself in Norway. Because I had started losing confidence in my ability of what I do. But sometimes, man, you just get tired of fighting and trying to prove yourself.

Ike Turner

All anything takes, really, is confidence.

Rachel Ward

You have a huge amount of confidence when you're younger, which slowly ebbs away for the rest of your life.

You think: 'No problem. I can do that. Why shouldn't I do it?'

Ian Hislop

You've got so much confidence if you start making big putts because you know you just need to hit the greens, and you've got yourself a good opportunity for the birdies.

Louis Oosthuizen

When political and business leaders tell the public - any public - 'We don't trust you to make the right decision' - they prejudice that electorate against the very proposals they want it to accept and undermine public confidence in themselves.

Preston Manning

As an athlete, confidence makes me more competitive and helps me perform better.

Marlen Esparza

This - the leadership of the mayor is crucial, because it is to the mayor that people will look to provide the vision, the energy, and the sense of confidence in the rebuilding and the recovery.

Marc Morial

I think it is important to maintain a sense of self and confidence, not letting either falter for the sake of a particular part or project, no matter how great it might be.

Fred Savage

When I was in my teens and 20s, I looked to older Italian and French women. They always seemed so incredibly attractive to me because of their confidence. And because their faces had evidence of age: lines, dark circles, and half-lidded eyes, it made that confidence so rebellious. And that was incredibly attractive to me.

Justine Bateman

Queen Paola and I will never forget the ties that have grown between the people and us during the course of the years. Thank you for your confidence, tokens of sympathy and support, sometimes even with a little criticism. We always loved you.

King Albert II

We don't see the global citizen as someone with no identity, but rather someone who has confidence and is proud of his culture and history - and... open to the modern world.

Mozah bint Nasser Al Missned

I really always felt that I was going to be an actress. I had a lot of confidence in the fact that I would do well from a very early age. I didn't know how tough the business is.

Susan Lucci

Our citizens will lose their confidence or trust in the values and principles of the international community, especially if our personal identity is denied.

Boris Trajkovski

With girls, there's an insecurity that starts early on. It hangs around them, like some annoying kid from down the block who won't take the hint and go home when dinnertime comes. And moms are usually not great at giving their daughters confidence.

Steve Schirripa

The school made it very clear that women were entitled to positions of authority. That sense of entitlement allowed us to feel that we have a natural place in leadership in the world. That gave me a mental and emotional confidence.

Linda Vester

Working out and working as an actor have gone hand in hand - I always feel more prepared if I know I have done a workout. It gives me confidence - and peace of mind.

Sebastian Stan

There's nothing like being a soldier for confidence or learning your limits or enduring utter humiliation.

Guy Davenport

It should strengthen investors' confidence. This is done through transparency, high quality financial reports, and a standardized economic market. This is not just for China, but also for the world market as a whole.

Richard Grasso

Don't take anything for granted. If you don't believe in yourself, nobody else will. Have a little more confidence.

Cathy Moriarty

Well, it seems to me a scientist has need for both vision and confidence.

Harry Essex

Future peace, prosperity and confidence depend not just on ourselves but on the success of all nations. Hence, we are all partners, no matter what our backgrounds, cultures, faiths and histories.

Hassanal Bolkiah

I've gradually gained more confidence swimming for distance in the open sea, but I still return to the rock pools.

Raymond Bonner

A sense of humor is important. I'm always attracted to a girl with confidence. In terms of looks, I don't have a type. I think a lot of girls think that they have to be super-thin, to meet the Hollywood image, but I think a girl who is voluptuous is very beautiful.

Corey Sevier

I'm sure that they will continue to look for ways to try and undermine my support, but I have every confidence that in doing this job for South Dakota, I will continue to build on my support and be able to succeed once again in November.

Stephanie Herseth

I had a great deal of confidence when I graduated from Berkeley. I had almost none when I was at Princeton. After a while, when people tell you you can't do something because you're a woman, you begin to believe maybe they're right.

Margaret Geller

As a football team, you head into the season the same way with confidence and a positive mindset that you are going to win a bunch of football games.

Matthew Stafford

Wherever I've been, and I've been to over 20, maybe 25, countries in Africa, I've noticed how their backbone is broken. They don't have any confidence in themselves. They always think a white man will solve their problems from outside for them.

Bunker Roy

Every girl/woman in the world has flaws. Instead of focusing on your flaws when you look in a mirror, focus on the parts of you that you love; try to do this every morning. You will ooze confidence all day long.

Chelan Simmons

I had the benefit of being guided by Lew Wasserman. I think part of being a mentor is you have to have confidence in the people you're guiding and mentoring.

Sidney Sheinberg

In common with many who have a brain injury, I initially lost my confidence and felt very vulnerable, as if a protective layer of skin had been stripped away.

Maryam D'Abo

Speaking from experience, because I have three daughters, I think it's always important to give your daughter the confidence that she needs so that she won't look elsewhere for approval and feeling love and acceptance.

David Charvet

I try very hard to maintain the confidence of my sources by speaking candidly with them, honoring agreements about the use of our conversation, and practicing journalism in an honest and straightforward way.

John Harwood

When the Strokes first started playing gigs, instead of getting into a costume for the shows, we talked about how we should dress every day, in real life, like we're playing onstage. I don't really care about clothes, but it's about wearing something that gives you social confidence. Or maybe helps you pick up chicks.

Julian Casablancas

Self confidence for me is a fragile fleece.

Sylvia Kristel

People of faith should be able to have confidence in their right to freely express and live their beliefs.

Donald Wuerl

When you're expected to win and you have the press saying that you are going to win the Olympic gold medal, and you're the only sure thing in the Olympics, it can undermine your confidence.

Scott Hamilton

People are slow to claim confidence in undertakings of magnitude.

Ovid

Having once decided to achieve a certain task, achieve it at all costs of tedium and distaste. The gain in self confidence of having accomplished a tiresome labor is immense.

Arthur Helps

Eight shows a week is daunting, and it can be terrifying. But it just instills such a sense of confidence and growth.

Brooke Shields

I think with actors, if you just don't set about trying to crush their confidence immediately, you're usually OK.

John Malkovich

I had my years of struggling. Some of my shows failed miserably, and I was upset by it and it dented my confidence. But I never stopped. I kept going for it.

Regis Philbin

Through first-class education, a generation marches down the long uncertain road of the future with confidence.

Wynton Marsalis

I state in my book 'Become Your Own Matchmaker,' confidence is the key to any endeavor. Women don't realize that when they do things they love and are passionate about - their confidence soars. Men are attracted to women who feel happy and decisive about life.

Patti Stanger

I didn't have that much confidence. Maybe it looks that

way. I'm glad it does.

Elia Kazan

Europe is a strong market for the U.S. If it has problems, if there's a lack of consumer confidence, if there's a deeper recession, this will deeply affect jobs in the U.S.

George Papandreou

My dad is a Jack Nicholson lookalike and a frustrated performer, my mother's into reading and poetry. I suppose the thing I owe them most is my confidence.

Michael Sheen

For me to even be talking about bikini confidence is crazy. If you had asked me a couple of months ago, I probably would have been like, 'what are you talking about...' so it's actually huge for me to even feel okay with putting a bikini on.

Jordin Sparks

I'm fairly competant as a director and actor, but I am Mr. Neurotic as a writer. I just don't have enough confidence in my abilities to take criticism well. I take it personally. Start with 'It's a masterpiece,' and then tell me what you think could be changed.

Tim Robbins

I think in the lifetime of a tennis player there are many times where you feel that tremendous confidence.

Gabriela Sabatini

My mother gave me a sense of independence, a sense of total confidence that we could do whatever it was we set out to do. That's how we were raised.

Robin Wright

Jay Z and President Bush have a lot in common, that same brash confidence.

Saul Williams

It turned out in the long run that Lincoln's credit and the popular confidence that supported it were as valuable both to his creditors and himself as if the sums which stood over his signature had been gold coin in a solvent bank.

John George Nicolay

Confidence is such a fragile and precious thing.

David Duval

The most important characteristic that has allowed me to succeed is confidence. I have always been comfortable in my own skin, and even when I was just starting out in my career, had the strength and self-assurance to ask tough questions and push for answers.

Heather Bresch

I'm a great believer in our ability to come up with the ideas necessary to solve the big questions. I have less confidence that we'll be able to find a consensus about which ones are right without experiment.

Leonard Susskind

There's no such thing as lack of confidence. You either have it or you don't.

Rob Andrew

Politics is an act of faith; you have to show some kind of confidence in the intellectual and moral capacity of the public.

George McGovern

The strongest bank in the United States will last only so long as the people will have sufficient confidence in it to keep their money there.

Carter G. Woodson

You go through those awkward, dorky, geeky stages, and growing up in the industry amplifies all that. Fortunately, I have a mother who encouraged me to build my confidence from within and embrace my imperfections.

Jurnee Smollett

Everybody wants to be somebody. The thing you have to do is give them confidence they can. You have to give a kid a dream.

George Foreman

It is best to act with confidence, no matter how little right you have to it.

Lillian Hellman

Confidence doesn't come out of nowhere. It's a result of something... hours and days and weeks and years of constant work and dedication.

Roger Staubach

My confidence is easy to shake. I am very well aware of all of my flaws. I am aware of all the insecurities that I have.

Taylor Swift

Greed is the lack of confidence of one's own ability to create.

Vanna Bonta

I have good and bad days like everyone else. I just try to be positive and surround myself with great people. When I think about all the great things and people I have had in my life, that gives me confidence.

Jessica White

Community service has taught me all kinds of skills and increased my confidence. You go out there and think on your feet, work with others and create something from nothing. That's what life's all about.

Andrew Shue

A fit body gives you confidence. And there's nothing more impressive than a great attitude, which you can wear on your sleeve. But you'll have to remember the difference between being rude and being confident.

Virat Kohli

If you improve a teacher's self-esteem, confidence, communication skills or stress levels, you improve that teacher's overall effectiveness across the curriculum.

Elaine MacDonald

I don't believe in team motivation. I believe in getting a team prepared so it knows it will have the necessary confidence when it steps on a field and be prepared to play a good game.

Tom Landry

The whole kiss-and-tell thing is a negative approach that often happens in a World Cup. We will see negative stories about the players and it can affect their confidence and the overall performance of the national team on the pitch, let alone the bid to actually stage the competition.

Gary Lineker

I think the most important thing about coaching is that you have to have a sense of confidence about what you're doing. You have to be a salesman, and you have to get your players, particularly your leaders, to believe in what you're trying to accomplish on the basketball floor.

Phil Jackson

When you disarm the people, you commence to offend them and show that you distrust them either through cowardice or lack of confidence, and both of these opinions generate hatred.

Niccolo Machiavelli

I'll never tell a lie. I'll never make a misleading statement. I'll never betray the confidence that any of you had in me. And I'll never avoid a controversial issue.

Jimmy Carter

I think I have an inner confidence that my tastes are pretty simple, that what I find funny finds a wide audience. I'm not particularly intellectual or clever or minority-focused in my creative instincts. And I'm certainly not aware of suppressing more sophisticated ambitions.

Rowan Atkinson

Leadership is a matter of having people look at you and gain confidence, seeing how you react. If you're in control, they're in control.

Tom Landry

Peace is not an absence of war, it is a virtue, a state of mind, a disposition for benevolence, confidence, justice.

Baruch Spinoza

The focus of tolerance education is to deal with the concept of equality and fairness. We need to establish confidence with children that there is more goodness than horror in this world.

Morris Dees

I think that everyone has something about themselves that they feel is their weakness... their 'disability.' And I'm certain we all have one, because I think of a disability as being anything which undermines our belief and confidence in our own abilities.

Aimee Mullins

The qualities I most admire in women are confidence and kindness.

Oscar de la Renta

Well, I am a Republican, and I would run as a Republican. And I have a lot of confidence in the Republican Party. I don't have a lot of confidence in the president. I think what's happening to this country is unbelievably bad. We're no longer a respected country.

Donald Trump

My confidence comes from the daily grind - training my butt off day in and day out.

Hope Solo

I think confidence is the most appealing quality in any human being or any artist; that's what really attracts us to people.

Marilyn Manson

When you have police officers who abuse citizens, you erode public confidence in law enforcement. That makes the job of good police officers unsafe.

Mary Frances Berry

Our daily deeds as ordinary South Africans must produce an actual South African reality that will reinforce humanity's belief in justice, strengthen its confidence in the nobility of the human soul, and sustain all our hopes for a glorious life for all.

Nelson Mandela

Confidence comes with maturity, being more accepting of yourself.

Nicole Scherzinger

As Americans, there are very few things we have confidence in.

Howard Schultz

I was a pretty insecure kid, didn't have a lot of friends, and was picked on a lot, and music gave me confidence.

Sarah McLachlan

And I love kick boxing. It's a lot of fun. It gives you a lot of confidence when you can kick somebody in the head.

Alicia Keys

You have to have confidence. You can't be someone who's so insecure that she's a basket case.

Kate Bosworth

Americans reading the paper, listening to the news every single day, and all you hear is things are getting worse and worse. And that has a psychological effect on consumer confidence. That's what consumer confidence is.

Howard Schultz

Even if consumer confidence hit rock bottom, that most likely would not be enough, by itself, to cause a depression.

Charles Duhigg

Temporary tax cuts don't create permanent confidence, nor permanent jobs.

Mark McKinnon

I think the Egyptian people need to restore confidence that Americans, the U.S., means what they say when they talk about democracy, rule of law.

Mohamed ElBaradei

My parents were there: in front of me, behind me, in the middle of my life at all times: reprimanding me, giving me confidence, teaching me valuable lessons, to help make me the man I am today.

Marcus Samuelsson

I am lucky, that is all. Lucky because there are a lot of people - producers, directors, people who buy tickets - who put confidence in me.

Antonio Banderas

I didn't have much confidence in myself... never.

Maurice Sendak

In college, I had a lot of friends who were writers and wanted to be writers and I felt intimidated by it. I just didn't know if I had any gift or voice and I had no confidence about it.

Rashida Jones

I'm just glad that my community has faith and confidence in me.

Charles B. Rangel

You think you have some stable talent that will show no matter what you're writing, and if it doesn't seem to be getting across to the audience once, you can't imagine that moment when it suddenly will. Gradually, gradually you gain that confidence.

Joan Didion

Being out of a job can erode people's confidence and their sense of possibility; and employers, often unfairly, tend to take long-term unemployment as a signal that something is wrong.

James Surowiecki

I have great confidence in Rick Caruso's unique qualifications and his ability to lead a successful bid for the Los Angeles Dodgers.

Joe Torre

Being funny, it turns out, is like being a bank. It's a confidence trick. As long as everyone believes in you, you are fine.

Evan Davis

A series of small but real accomplishments gives people the energy and confidence to continue. For instance, a person who wants to write a novel might resolve to write one sentence each day. Or a person who wants to start running might resolve to run for one minute.

Gretchen Rubin

People have no confidence that Washington, both sides of aisle, are coming together to try and do what's right for the economy.

Michael Bloomberg

The Achilles Heel of the Americas was the lack of cultural confidence typical of new settlers.

Arthur Erickson

A vote of confidence from Cisco Systems can be very important to fledging technology companies, especially if they have initial public offerings on the horizon.

Alex Berenson

I want to find the candidates who understand the principles of American exceptionalism and have the character, the courage, and the confidence to actually lead the greatest nation in the world.

Jim DeMint

False shame accompanies a man that is poor, shame that either harms a man greatly or profits him; shame is with poverty, but confidence with wealth.

Hesiod

If you're asked something on a movie set and you say 'I don't know,' you lose confidence in every department. What you need to say is 'I'll have that for you in five minutes.'

Mike Birbiglia

One of the areas I have a little less confidence in is giving any kind of a speech.

Danica Patrick

Experts said public companies worry about the loss of customer confidence and the legal liability to shareholders or security vendors when they report flaws.

Barton Gellman

I think the best directors provide you with a safe environment where they can instill you with confidence and allow you to try things out and not feel like you're failing or that you're doing it wrong.

Luke Evans

Having lived a full and stimulating life before I had my kids, I've relished every minute I've had to spend with them and felt a degree of confidence in dealing with their trials and tribulations to date.

Mariella Frostrup

Once the public loses confidence in a president's leadership at a time of war, once they don't trust him anymore, once his credibility is sharply diminished, how does he get it back?

Robert Dallek

It's a confidence booster for me to be known as a female who can take on any action, which is nice, to have that reputation, because then people know that when they hire me, I can actually do the physical stuff.

Rachel Nichols

Ed Sullivan brought me to TV first in 1952, then Garry Moore's program gave me a lot of confidence and freedom.

Alan King

My kids are incredibly secure. More and more of their friends' parents are divorcing, but my kids have absolute confidence that we'll stay together forever. That goes a long, long way.

Ayelet Waldman

If you don't have the confidence in baking, commit to making the recipe three times. The first two, do it exactly the way I've told you to make it. Twice. The first time you'll screw it up. The second time it will come out pretty good, and then the third time, make your adjustments.

Tom Douglas

Mastering one recipe is better than mastering too many. Learn something and own it, and you'll feel so much better about it. You'll have more confidence if you've made it five times, and that confidence adds so much fun to cooking.

Tom Douglas

The problem with the auto industry is layered upon the lack of consumer confidence. People are not buying cars. I don't care whether they're or American cars, or international cars.

Jennifer Granholm

The route of expropriation, and especially in energy matters, is not what most promotes investment or generates greater confidence.

Enrique Pena Nieto

When girls feel bad about their looks, 60 percent avoid normal daily activities like raising their hand in class or even going to the doctor. That means that girls do not show up for life when they don't feel good enough or pretty enough. A role model can help girls see beauty as a source of confidence, not anxiety.

Mandy Moore

I should like to think how we write as theologians would reflect our confidence in the One who makes that writing possible. That is one of the reasons, moreover, that the scriptures remain paradigmatic for how we are to write.

Stanley Hauerwas

I write all the time, but you just want to be careful what you put out. That's all. You want to have the confidence that you've done what you need to do to it, because otherwise it's an exercise in vanity.

Dylan Moran

I have derived enormous confidence from being a husband and father.

Julian Fellowes

The confidence is there, the game is there, but physically you can't fight nature sometimes. You can't do much about it.

Novak Djokovic

I've never done anything so political before. I've spent years shouting my mouth off about serious issues over dinner tables but never really had the confidence to express my views in a song.

George Michael

I see nothing that points to a recession in Germany. But I see considerable long-term tasks ahead of us that have to do with markets regaining confidence in Europe and that have a lot to do with reducing debt.

Angela Merkel

It doesn't matter if you are model or not; confidence is something that comes from inside.

Erin Heatherton

I'd be lying if I said I had confidence in every choice I've made, that I have faith in every film I do on every shot.

Ethan Hawke

I had no confidence at school. I was not a good student and I really thought I was pretty stupid. Just dumb.

Tommy Hilfiger

I'm convinced that quite a lot of young people, when they get in trouble with the law, it's a cry for help there. Because it's not that they go out to offend. It's that their behaviour is self-parading, it's the big 'I'. And sometimes that means they're really lacking in confidence.

David Blunkett

Acting's all about the confidence you exude, especially on film. I mean, nervousness isn't attractive in anyone, but a film camera will seek it out and punish you.

John C. Reilly

With movies, so much of it is, 'Who is the human being that is going to be directing it?' Because it is their medium. In a way, you are serving the director, and when it is someone that you feel you can have a lot of confidence in, it can make a big difference.

Annette Bening

The fight for reform comes down to a simple goal: giving our citizens the confidence that government serves the people first and the people only.

Bob Riley

You couldn't give me any more confidence than when I

was on T.V. because I was in control, but I wasn't in control in my private life.

Cilla Black

On the first day of school, my father told me I'd be the most popular girl and everyone would love me and want to be my friend. It wasn't so, but it gave me an enormous amount of confidence.

Maeve Binchy

Learning how to relive again on life's terms sure doesn't do much for your confidence. You have to kind of walk in faith that the next step is going to be just a little bit better than the last step.

Joe Nichols

I've been fortunate to be working mostly right out of school. Every year, there was a little something, and it kept the confidence going. It's about confidence and the belief.

Oscar Isaac

Hip-hop is all about impact, baby. You can sell records,

you can be two-times platinum, you can be gold... but if you lame, you lame, man. We try to provide the exact opposite of that. It's style, individuality, confidence. We exude that.

Wale

You may be right that people say: 'You know what, we had Obama. He was inexperienced. The guy had great rhetoric, sounded good, looked good, but has turned out to be an utter disaster. I want someone where I have confidence and credibility that they're up to the job and that I can trust what they tell me.'

Karl Rove

The crowd gives us so much energy and we are able to really feed off of it. Hitting those shots and having the crowd go crazy helps boost our confidence. We love our fans.

Steve Nash

Rugby gave me a confidence. I was quite shy and relatively timid, but it gave me the confidence to be a little bit more out-going and back myself a bit more.

Brian O'Driscoll

I like the idea of an open, international London that thrives on attracting hard-working, talented people but has the confidence to tell them they must play by the same rules as everyone else.

Mohsin Hamid

I'm not comparing myself with anyone, but I am very confident about my captaincy, as I have already led India and in the IPL also. I have confidence I can bring out each player's ability fully and also give them a lot of confidence... I would like to stick to what I know best and what I have confidence in.

Virat Kohli

The usual channels of university studies or secretarial work did not appeal to me. I cherished difficult dreams through confidence in myself.

Ella Maillart

You don't find women with great confidence dressed as if they don't care.

Trinny Woodall

I'm playing one of the principal roles, which gives you more clout and more confidence.

Charles Dance

I have confidence that the Unitarian Church will steadily grow and will help to sustain many of my fellow citizens in these important days that lie ahead of us.

Leverett Saltonstall

Turning 50 can be difficult, sometimes dangerous, for women. The danger is in that blip that can come from the fact that you become invisible, and if you're not careful and don't embrace that, it can trip you up and you lose confidence.

Dawn French

This is how I define grace: you're on the main stage, and it looks like it has been rehearsed 100 times, everything goes so smoothly. That's where I get my confidence and success, from knowing that I have an edge because I know I'm prepared.

Alex Rodriguez

If a cream can give you confidence then you really have to check your whole confidence department in the first place.

Freida Pinto

Alan Whicker may be the last Briton to have worn a silver-buttoned blazer with complete confidence.

Craig Brown

If we will maintain our hope and confidence in the genius of our people, they will work out this problem, and their ability and industry will bring us back to normal conditions.

Frank B. Kellogg

The confidence that we Indians are suddenly infused with while doing something wrong is absolutely commendable.

Kailash Kher

I have watched lives change. I have seen women gain confidence.

Amanda Lindhout

My confidence came from the way I grew up, and I'm grateful for it.

Amanda Lindhout

Lack of confidence - every time I start a new piece of work, it seems I have to spend a long while under the duvet thinking I can't do it.

Sue Townsend

I love Tina Turner. I'm one of Tina Turner's biggest fans. Tina Turner was a big influence on me to become a singer. A role model and in a way she gave me back my confidence in choosing my material.

Bonnie Tyler

I think that you do get a little extra jolt of confidence when you win an Emmy.

Edie Falco

There's a confidence that comes from youth and not knowing better. But there comes a point, as an actor, when you do know better, and that is when the fear starts.

Kiefer Sutherland

Nothing improves your confidence and brings a team together more than winning a cup.

Gary Neville

You can't lose your concentration at all. And there are times when you're on the stage, and you've got silence, which is wonderful, but you have to have the confidence to make you realize it's fine. You can't suddenly wobble and think, 'They're not interested.'

John Hurt

Psych yourself up until you're confident that the world will be interested in what happens to your characters. Confidence is key.

Deborah Moggach

I think that my father would find it so confusing that people want to imitate him. Not because he didn't have confidence in who he was, but because he never imitated anybody. He was his own person.

Patti Davis

By the way, the secret of speaking French is confidence.
Whether you are right or wrong, you don't hesitate.

Joseph Epstein

AT&T Park, chalk it up. This is a great pitcher's park, great
weather. It's a great place to pitch. It's all positive and no
negative. You can go out and challenge guys. I've got the
confidence to attack the strike zone and not nibble so much.

Tim Hudson

I believe good governments have nothing to hide. We want
to ensure we maintain confidence in our public institutions.

Jay Weatherill

You can't be minimalist as a director until you have
acquired the experience and confidence to say no.

Richard Eyre

At times of distress, we all like to recall the advice of fathers and mothers. The best advice my father gave me was to keep faith and deep confidence in the potential of the Greek people; nurture the belief that they can do things.

George Papandreou

I am determined to honour the confidence which has been extended to us by the people of our great land. And I say to all of those who have voted for us today, I say to each and every one of them that I will be a prime minister for all Australians.

Kevin Rudd

The Pulitzer Prize is an idea; it's a vote of confidence. Like literature, it exists purely in the mind.

Jeffrey Eugenides

If you can hit your 3- and 5-woods with confidence from the fairway, par 5s become birdie opportunities, and 420-yard par 4s are a lot less scary.

Ernie Els

I did a lot of ridiculous television. Between 1980 and '85 I had no confidence, so I did everything I was told to do.

Dana Carvey

I grew up thinking anything was possible simply because of seeing women in power - like, you know, running the country. Which is a thought that continues to give Americans indigestion... Direction is about having a vision, but the practice of being a director is a con game - a confidence game.

Mira Nair

I was very interested in that. It is very important to have confidence as well as to build up experience.

Alain Prost

With new jobs, new ideas, and growing confidence that our brightest days lie ahead, Wisconsin is on the move.

Jim Doyle

Not hippie - my parents were not hippies - but they were very supportive and encouraging, and that does a lot for someone, and it gives them a lot of confidence.

Jenna Elfman

I actually like pole dancing! It gives you so much confidence. I never thought I'd do it, but now I'm really into it.

Taylor Schilling

Yet you should practice the greatest possible love and confidence in treating with Him.

Alphonsus Liguori

I'm attracted to men who just love what they do, have confidence in what they do and have potential to be on their own if they need to be.

Nadine Velazquez

For investor confidence, it is important that there is certainty about the future of Ireland in E.U.

Jose Manuel Barroso

My advice is very simple: if you can win a small battle, it gives you confidence in the political process to take on bigger battles, and so it is very much a bottom-up grass-roots way of doing politics.

David Miliband

If you're too embarrassed and want to hide behind your computer screen, that's what this is for. It's about building confidence and that's what U by Kotex does. Girls owning their bodies and health.

Khloe Kardashian

Confidence comes from within and as long as you are putting forth a respectable effort to take good care of yourself, you should feel confident about that path.

Stacy Keibler

To have family behind you who love you more than words can say gives you so much confidence, because it allows you to go off and be who you want to be.

Cat Deeley

It is evident that not all people that have the confidence of the prime minister are the same ones that have the confidence of the head of state.

Jose Eduardo Dos Santos

I am not comfortable telling people I am trying stand-up because to me that implies confidence. I'm - well, I'm not.

Jessie Cave

You start to think bigger when you see how quickly a TV show can catch on in a whole country. That confidence, and thinking big, opened a lot of doors.

Andrew Shue

I am running for my Senate district in 2014 and looking forward hopefully to earning the confidence of my community once again and being reelected for that seat.

Wendy Davis

The first time I had to hold a baby, I was really nervous, but I soon grew in confidence.

Jessica Raine

Magic is the oldest part of the show business profession. It can now be used as a forward-thinking tool to build a child's confidence. It has been an amazing part in many entertainers' lives, including Steve Martin and the late Johnny Carson.

Criss Angel

Eventually, the tribe developed so much confidence in me that they invited me to be their chieftain.

Roland Joffe

When I became a Christian my confidence grew.

Cliff Richard

Ronald Reagan's vision of smaller government, less taxes, and a strong national defense has led to a prosperous America. As president, he rebuilt our military and reinvigorated our confidence in ourselves.

David Vitter

What would a loss of confidence in the dollar actually look

like? Gold going absolutely nuts.

Paul Singer

There comes a time in the history of nations when their peoples must become fully reconciled to their past if they are to go forward with confidence to embrace their future.

Kevin Rudd

Go on - but don't think you can kill my confidence. I've had experts doing it for years.

John Osborne

There is so much pressure to be thin, and you constantly compare yourself to others. But confidence is something that comes with age and experience - it has to be earned along the way.

Cherie Lunghi

I believe veganism can be beneficial for the individual and the world, and of course the animal, but belief is like laying in the dark with someone and telling them you love them and hearing nothing back. So I've never had the confidence to get on a soapbox and tell someone else what to do.

Casey Affleck

I was lucky I was raised by parents who gave me a lot of sense of self and a lot of confidence in myself.

Sprague Grayden

President Bush offers the American people an optimistic vision and a clear choice in November. The President has provided steady leadership in remarkably changing times. He knows exactly where he wants to lead this country, and he has complete confidence in the American people.

Henry Bonilla

I have also noticed that when a rider who had confidence in his ability was defeated, after doing his level best to win, always received an ovation from the gathering.

Major Taylor

Footballers are the most vulnerable people. They exude confidence, but inside, they're so lacking in confidence. They know they can lose form or be injured. This profession is so insecure, you wouldn't believe it.

Gordon Taylor

Without rebuilding the confidence between parties, you will never succeed.

Harri Holkeri

The first album I started out, I just did everything completely alone. I think it has to do with confidence. The more confidence you develop in your own sound, the more you can open up and alchemize that with other people, just set it free, and not feel challenged by that.

Bat for Lashes

I think that I have never had the confidence to really aggressively get behind myself, and so what I do tends to be - I don't want to say 'sheepish,' but there is a sheepish quality to my ability to toot my own horn. I'm very Midwestern in that way. So I just do what I like to do, and what I think I do well is not very loud, necessarily.

Kathryn Erbe

However, I must say that I am very happy to see that we have such a positive result for our first referendum in our history and that gives me more confidence in Taiwan's democracy.

Chen Shui-bian

As I said, I began losing confidence in my instincts, which is tough and very bad for an instinctive person.

Kim Novak

I'm glad I made business investments, because it gave me the confidence financially to make brave choices. If I hadn't done that, I'd still have been trying to play 19-year-olds in films. I know there are other avenues for me.

Preity Zinta

What I learned about stammering was that, when as a young child you lose the confidence of anyone who wants to listen to you, you lose confidence in your voice and the right to speech. And a lot of the therapy was saying, 'You have a right to be heard.'

Tom Hooper

I guess confidence is the only thing that I take from project to project, but I'm always open to learning everybody's style - the director, the actor I'm working with.

Freida Pinto

When I'm dancing, I don't know where the confidence comes from, but I just pretend I'm someone else, I think, and then I go out and dance.

Maisie Williams

I have implicit faith in Sun Yat-sen, not because I am his blind follower, but because he really arouses the deepest respect in everybody. I do not know of another person in China who has such a broad and international outlook, whose ideas are so constructive, and who has such deep faith and confidence in his own mission.

Chiang Kai-shek

I am always drawn to men that are funny. I do not know why. But I am always drawn to people that are struggling with parts of themselves... But it's like in the end, there has to be confidence.

Vanessa Carlton

Winning Wimbledon was a great feeling and it is still a great feeling. It has given me so much confidence.

Goran Ivanisevic

I thank all of those deputies who supported the government and gave it a vote of confidence. I believe each of those votes represents a responsible decision to avoid placing our country's membership of the eurozone in danger.

Lucas Papademos

I don't read reviews if I know in advance they're negative, because I can't have my confidence undermined when I'm writing.

Christopher Moore

I presumed the president was being truthful until a series of events undercut that confidence.

Bob Graham

I don't consider myself to be incredibly confident, or really lacking in confidence. When you're on Jonathan Ross' or

Graham Norton's show, inevitably there's something to sell. And there's a live audience; you're sat between Cameron Diaz and Tinie Tempah - I don't really see it as 'me.' It would be odd if it was.

James Corden

On stage, you have to have incredible confidence, or you would stop doing it. But I don't think I will ever get to the point where I go, 'I know exactly what I am doing,' and I don't think I want to.

James Corden

One of the biggest gifts you can give a child is confidence, because confidence will take you miles - more than talent, more than anything else. So yes, I want my children to have confidence and to be kind.

Rafe Spall

My first performance was in second grade with my friend Rodney Fisher, and we worked up versions of 'Long Tall Texan' and 'I Want to Hold Your Hand.' It gave me a little early confidence that I could actually do this music thing.

Lyle Lovett

Living in New York, you get a lot of confidence; when I go back to Michigan, I realise how obnoxious and demanding and straightforward I am.

Angel Haze

Being the youngest of five, you're adored, you're fueled with confidence.

Martin Short

It used to be that a son could look at the father, and pretty much know what life was gonna be like as an adult. There was confidence in that, and comfort in that, and frustration also.

Clancy Brown

Writers always have confidence issues - it comes with the territory. We never know where we fit in, or what the actual value of our work might be. So we hit lulls, or slogs. Throw in the idea that many creative people are somewhat manic-depressive, and it can get pretty dark at times.

R. A. Salvatore

I think swagger's a confidence. It's a confidence of you knowing that you work hard for your success. A lot of times, you can't develop swagger if you haven't worked hard to succeed.

Amar'e Stoudemire

Any new producer starting up is to get investors' confidence. Investors are still very very wary of anything to do with the arts world.

Ann Macbeth

Realizing full well that fine condition and confidence will not in themselves make a champion, it is my belief, however, that they are essential factors.

Major Taylor

Even when disco went out, I could still make hits. Once I had so much success, every idea became concentrated. I had so much confidence. I knew how the bass should sound, what rhythms would work. The tempos I knew: 110 to 120 BPM. I knew they would dance in the clubs in New York or anywhere.

Giorgio Moroder

I remember when I was a dancer and I had to do this performance and I was really nervous about it, and I happened at that moment to go see 'Flashdance.' I mean, it's silly, but I walked out of that movie going 'what a feeling!' I walked out with confidence.

Melissa Rosenberg

The crisis in Europe has affected the U.S. economy by acting as a drag on our exports, weighing on business and consumer confidence, and pressuring U.S. financial markets and institutions.

Ben Bernanke

Everything I do, I build a kind of confidence net - 'I'm able to execute this; it's fine.'

Dev Hynes

Thanks to President Bush and Republican principles, businesses now have more confidence to hire workers.

John Doolittle

I see success as bringing some confidence back to the American people that despite our differences, we can find some ways to move forward.

Patty Murray

I mean, if you are directing actors to do one thing and then directing them to do something else entirely because the one thing you wanted them to do may not work, then you are just shattering their confidence in the project.

Atom Egoyan

It was a great time here in the States this year, and definitely I feel like I'm playing well again. I gained a lot of confidence in the last couple of weeks, and I just have to, you know, keep going and keep the momentum now.

Daniela Hantuchova

Right now I have more confidence in myself. I grew up.

Amelie Mauresmo

I do find my speech difficult at times, but it's getting so

much better as my confidence grows and that's thanks to the position I'm now in, which is totally due to my fans.

Gareth Gates

The world isn't one way or another. Things can be changed very, very rapidly by someone with sufficient confidence, sufficient knowledge and sufficient authority.

Rory Stewart

This was all very new to me and I did not want to ruin his film! So we worked hard on that basis of confidence that is needed to collaborate comfortably.

Helena Christensen

I've refined my mechanics, refined my pitches. I've gotten more confidence, and I've gotten more determination. I've got a better idea what I'm doing out there.

Randy Johnson

If you serve well, your volleys are going to be so much easier. It has got to do with confidence, obviously.

Stefan Edberg

I gain a lot of confidence through study.

Autumn Reeser

I emphasize... that the Harrimans showed great courage and loyalty and confidence in us, because three or four of us were really running the business, the day to day business.

Prescott Bush

The 12 years I was in Fleetwood Mac before were not particularly happy years. I was not in a very good place, psychologically, when I left. I didn't have a lot of confidence in what I was doing.

Lindsey Buckingham

The only investable idea I have real confidence in is farming and forestry. My family owns some forest, and now we're closing on a farm. Make the farming more sustainable and the forestry more sustainable, and everyone benefits.

Jeremy Grantham

To be let go from a soap opera is the most embarrassing confidence basher in the world. It's like, 'Oh, if I'm not good enough for that, I'm not good enough for anything.'

Cam Gigandet

I have so many single girlfriends who fit themselves into the mold of what they think a guy's looking for. But being comfortable around men is about being comfortable with yourself. They gravitate toward confidence. Really, that is what they want to be around.

Cobie Smulders

As to the question of elected or not elected, each member of the European Commission has been appointed jointly by the governments of the 15 member states, and undergone individual scrutiny and a vote of confidence from the European Parliament.

Mario Monti

Such evidence is not the only kind which produces belief; though positivism maintains that it is the only kind which ought to produce so high a degree of confidence as all minds have or can be made to have through their agreements.

Chauncey Wright

I came into the 'Comedy Bang! Bang!' TV show with a level of confidence that I don't think I would've had if I hadn't been doing the podcast for three years already. I certainly had to figure out in those three years the sense of humor I wanted to do and the way to talk to celebrities without being incredibly intimidated by them.

Scott Aukerman

The oldest pitcher acquires confidence in his ballclub - he doesn't try to do it all himself.

Burleigh Grimes

Like my hero Virginia Woolf, I do lack confidence. I always find that the novel I'm finishing, even if it's turned out fairly well, is not the novel I had in my mind. I think a lot of writers must negotiate this, and if they don't admit it, they're not being honest.

Michael Cunningham

We want to encourage the young ones to learn and get some confidence in sports. It's fun and keeps you active and moving.

Christine Taylor

Old Etonians are the most charming people in the world. It's not just the analytic ability and the great education; there is a really easy confidence to them that draws people to them and makes their passage though the world a little easier.

Laura Wade

The once-unthinkable loss of the AAA rating will constitute a further hit to already fragile business and consumer confidence.

Mohamed El-Erian

I find that all great directors, and I would include Ben Affleck and Clint Eastwood in that, they have great confidence. And with great confidence comes great freedom for the actor.

Amy Ryan

I think 'tradition' is in the past - and how can someone

really 'fear' a color? A man may prefer navy to turquoise, but a self assured man could wear any color and he knows that. It's a distinction of confidence.

Jean Pigozzi

All my family were brilliant cooks when I was growing up, but I ended up just cleaning up, so I've always lacked confidence in the kitchen.

Amanda Eliasch

When I took my first job, I was among only a handful of women. It was isolating at times. My love for technology kept me going, and I got to where I am today driven by my passion and self confidence.

Padmasree Warrior

Our expanding Canadian operations are concrete evidence of General Motors confidence in Canada.

Charles E. Wilson

Not to be too preachy, but I would really recommend to people, if you get the chance, to trust yourselves to leap without a net, because that will build the confidence. You know, you might shock yourself with how much you don't need a net because you can catch yourself.

Ross Mathews

I lack confidence as an actor.

Charles Durning

I lack confidence, but I've been so lucky the way jobs have come to me, and I'm so grateful for them. I know how many brilliant actors there are out there who aren't getting the chances. While the work is there, I will grab it with both hands. It could all end tomorrow. You never know what's around the corner.

Sheridan Smith

I'd never been a tract writer; I'd never been a philosopher; I'd never taken part in extraordinary industrial dispute activism; I'd not been in any of that background, but I was able to mix it in what had become, conceived to be, the new front line of politics - the ability on television to convey confidence and assurance without saying anything.

David Lange

I think there's a kind of confidence I often feel when I'm writing that I don't feel when I'm in the world, I guess. I feel a different kind of conviction about my choices. I feel much more insecure and awkward in the world, somehow, than I do when I'm writing.

Karen Russell

I had gained so much confidence through my college achievements that I wanted to tackle the world.

Donna Rice

I didn't act professionally before going to drama school. I don't know if I had the confidence. I didn't think I'd get in when I first auditioned for drama school, and then I did.

Francois Arnaud

I thought I was attractive when I shot 'My Big Fat Greek Wedding.' Studio executives and movie reviewers let me know I had a confidence in my looks that was not shared by them.

Nia Vardalos

The bottom line in my view is that America's mothers and fathers deserve to have confidence in law enforcement's ability to ensure that their children are being raised in the safest possible environment.

Bob Ney

But I do think the survey group - and I think Charlie Duelfer is a great leader. I have the utmost confidence in Charles. I think you will get as full an answer as you can possibly get.

David Kay

I'd always put on little shows at home, but when I was 11, I did a community event in Woodford, where anyone could go. You had three days of vocal training and performed your song at the end. I sang 'I Say a Little Prayer.' It's a tough song to sing but they gave me the confidence to go for it and belt it out.

Naomi Scott

I think people are always like, 'She's a model-turned-actress.' And I don't want to turn actress. I want to do both. I wouldn't have built the confidence to do acting if I didn't model.

Dree Hemingway

I always try to keep the confidence of the actors, and try my best to make them feel comfortable or confident.

Sean Durkin

I wanted to make comics that get at feelings that connect to the deepest moments of our lives, reading Tolstoy, Flaubert, Flannery O'Connor, Herman Melville, William Faulkner, Vladimir Nabokov and Carver to help gain the confidence to figure it out. I knew, however, the most doomed approach would be to simply create stories that felt 'literary.'

Chris Ware

I believe the public's confidence would be increased if the federal government took over the functions of airport security screening for all passengers.

David Neeleman

From 1836, down to last year, there is no proof of the

Government having any confidence in the duration of peace, or possessing increased security against war.

Richard Cobden

Seeing how those companies operate, it didn't amount to a massive vote of confidence in their artists. There was talk of me going to Columbia after that, but nothing happened. I got disillusioned, and I pulled back.

Madeleine Peyroux

When I was younger, I was nervous and didn't have a huge amount of confidence as an actor. Comedy is something - you know when you're getting it right because you can hear. And you can hear if you're not getting it right! I like to create interesting, weird characters, and they're often best in comedies.

Lucy Punch

I wasn't a perfect thing at 17. I didn't have confidence. I was hunched over and real embarrassed, and I didn't want to be in the limelight. But it changed over time.

Lindsay Davenport

As long as I have that support from my team, and I have that confidence in myself that I train really hard, I think there's no one out there who can defeat me in my weight class.

Nonito Donaire

The confidence is really driven by the woman - whether she can have the confidence that there will be enough earning or income to finance all the domestic spending - but also by the middle-income class, which for many Asian countries has become the growth power for the economy.

Sri Mulyani Indrawati

I think just being on 'One Tree Hill' has given me a lot of confidence.

Kate Voegele

Tim Robbins had real confidence in college. He literally stole actors from the theater department at UCLA to be in his plays. The department heads got so mad at him.

Daphne Zuniga

On a personal note I want to gain more confidence and give back in any way I can.

Skylar Laine

I'm now wearing suits on stage, so I've kinda stepped up my game as far as image. Which I have to admit is kind of a pain the butt, but it's fun. It gives you a certain amount of confidence to walk on stage and look nice, but I can't say that I'm totally buying into the whole image factor.

Christopher Cross

I haven't always been good at flirting, but I've learned that flirting is all about confidence. I don't think it's about being sexy at all; it's just about having enough confidence to walk up to somebody and have a conversation with them.

Sevyn Streeter

Confidence, knowing for certain that the person making the call has your safety foremost in their mind. And knowing that the job you are about to take on is the right thing to do, that it makes sense.

Paul Gleason

I don't think anyone's sexuality needs to be a public issue other than to give others the confidence to love themselves wholeheartedly and to be their true, authentic self without any shame.

Crystal Bowersox

I struggled quite a long time with my backhand, which was one of my best weapons before my surgery. It took me a long time until I regained full confidence in it again and only tried to keep the ball in play at the start of the '09 season.

Marco Chiudinelli

In international or national crises, there are always questions of lack of confidence. You have to change the minds of the people in order to get results.

Harri Holkeri

I feel strongly that degrees are really valuable to people, and having MOOCs allow for credit down the line will increase the number of students with the confidence and wherewithal to complete degrees.

Daphne Koller

If I want to average 32 points a game, I can do that easily. It's just eight, eight, eight, eight. No problem. I can do that anytime. That's not being cocky. That's confidence.

Patrick Ewing

Working as a teaboy may have helped my confidence, but not everyone else was so pleased. I could never remember who had milk or how many sugars, and I had an unusual talent for spilling tea on the recording console.

Rick Astley

Denzel Washington invoked confidence. When you have confidence, you can do anything. And that's what happened. I learned about being honest and keeping it true, keeping it true in my performance.

Derek Luke

When you have a lot of construction going on, it sends a message of vitality that builds up consumer confidence. It gets people to spend money when they see that energy, that things are happening.

Mick Cornett

It definitely helps to have been through the arm training flow before and to have used the arm on orbit, and it also gives me the confidence to know that our training facilities are really good, that when you get up there, you feel like you've been there.

Linda M. Godwin

I love those films where I feel the director's confidence - where he doesn't need to overdo it with the shots and the cuts.

Jean-Marc Vallee

I have done a few roles that I've never watched, and if I happen to be flicking through channels and one pops up, I quickly move on. It's hard enough to sustain some self confidence without being reminded of things we'd rather not revisit but, in the end, it comes with the territory.

Terry O'Quinn

Before the season begins, I had even damaged some frames, but Ken did not hold it against me and kept all his confidence. He was the one who incontestably changed my life, because without his help, I do not know what I will have become.

Jacky Ickx

Investor confidence in Adani is fairly high, and most of our investors are long-term investors.

Gautam Adani

I become a better actor after I step on a stage in front of, like, 500 people when it's just me, a microphone and my guitar. You don't get as nervous walking into a room in front of 3 or 4 people and to do a scene or to walk on a set. You gain confidence.

Bryan Greenberg

At this time I had complete confidence in Russian policy and believed that the Western Allies deliberately allowed Germany and Russia to fight each other to death.

Klaus Fuchs

Everybody wants to be a star right now, to be heard, to have a voice, so you have to give the confidence for people to have that ability - and give them the wardrobe to become a star.

Zac Posen

There is not much we can say with absolute confidence about the early church, but we can be fairly sure that the first Christians would not have dreamed of making a likeness of Jesus.

Neil MacGregor

Now, honestly, every movie set that I go on, I walk onto set with the confidence that there is nothing that they can throw at me that's gonna surprise me.

Emily Watson

Our ad campaign with Pfizer is educational. Lipitor is the most widely prescribed drug in the country. For every prescription, there is a doctor writing it. It's a huge vote of confidence.

Robert Jarvik

I look forward to continuing to be a role model to women across the country and helping them have confidence in all they do in the ring, on the court or in the game of life!

Marlen Esparza

I haven't seen a player in this game, as long as I've been in it, that can't be pitched to... Barry is an outstanding ballplayer. I respect him an awful lot. I also have confidence in my pitchers that they can pitch to Barry Bonds and get him out.

Frank Robinson

I used to be so hard on myself. So hard on myself. Just my own worst critic to the nth degree. Absolutely undermining my confidence in every moment. Bad tape in my head all the time.

Bellamy Young

I don't have much of an ego, but I have a great deal of confidence!

Raymond Burr

What's beautiful about the actual acting class environment is that you can use it to push through everything: push your voice, push your inhibitions, push your fears, push your confidence, push your vulnerability, push your silences.

Dawn Olivieri

I'm a happy member of the church. I'm proud of it and defend it. It makes me bold and gives me confidence. I feel I know the answer to life - that it's all about. If you're not searching for the answer to life, you have more time to make art. It's a rock for me upon which I can tap dance.

Catherine Hicks

I also believe that it's the right thing to do, to maintain strong consumer confidence in our food systems. And I believe that the consumer should have strong confidence in our food systems.

Ann Veneman

Oddly, because she has that confidence, the people around her like her more. She becomes more a part of the Reaper family, and she also is able to get along with people more outside of their circle as well.

Ellen Muth

When you live in an environment where you aren't allowed to be fully who you are, you aren't taken seriously, and you aren't respected. What that actually does to a person's confidence and psyche is really fascinating to me.

Andre Holland

In my case, the long gaps between my books have got quite a lot to do with lack of confidence. A lot of the time when I'm not writing I start thinking I can't do it.

Wendy Cope

Well, I was coming off of being on 'Law & Order,' and I was a little worried that it might be the end of my career - I've never been one of those actors with a lot of confidence that the next good job will come along.

Jeremy Sisto

To be a good model, I'd need a lot more confidence... and more confidence to be more bare.

Jill Hennessy

I love to have confidence, but that confidence doesn't come

from myself. It comes from God, and that's what I wanted America to see.

Ashthon Jones

I think musicians oftentimes have the right skill set to be good actors. And with Rihanna, I noticed her and knew of her obviously, and was very taken with her charisma and her confidence.

Peter Berg

The only way to get back the confidence is to play and win matches. You can practise as much as you like, but you need confidence that comes from playing and winning matches.

Greg Rusedski

There's a physicality and confidence to Americans; they're very present. That's something I enjoy being around because it rubs off on you.

Ioan Gruffudd

There should be more interaction and more confidence

building between our various academic institutions just like how there needs to be a confidence building between industry and academics.

Pallam Raju

Being in Loyola College exposed me to other options and gave me confidence, apart from the freedom to bunk classes. I became a merchandiser and then a garment manufacturer, and interacting with foreign buyers and manufacturing foreign brands in India gave me a high.

Suriya

It is important that the Iraqi people have confidence in the election results and that the voting process, including the process for vote counting, is free and fair.

Zalmay Khalilzad

Eliminating the Death Tax will continue to restore consumer confidence, spur capital investment, and create new jobs which are critical components of economic growth, particularly within the small business community.

Howard Coble

Too often, investors are the target of fraudulent schemes disguised as investment opportunities. As you know, if the balance is tipped to the point where investors are not confident that there are appropriate protections, investors will lose confidence in our markets, and capital formation will ultimately be made more difficult and expensive.

Mary Schapiro

Our cattlemen have given us the safest, most abundant, most affordable beef supply in the world and I trust their judgment. And if you look at consumer confidence in this country, so does the American public.

Norm Coleman

Nature hath given not only to the highest, but also to the inferior, classes of the people of this nation, a boldness and confidence in speaking and answering, even in the presence of their princes and chieftains.

Giraldus Cambrensis

I think 'Sightseers' was a bit of an epiphany, a massive learning curve, and it gave me loads of confidence to go out there, and also to create a female character which is completely unexpected and defies convention.

Alice Lowe

A sense of humor is important. I'm always attracted to a girl with confidence. In terms of looks, I don't have a type.

Corey Sevier

The finished product is often of less importance than the skills and confidence gained through the process and the way in which the community is strengthened through people in it work and are brought together.

Ben Edwards

We must keep on trying to solve problems, one by one, stage by stage, if not on the basis of confidence and cooperation, at least on that of mutual toleration and self-interest.

Lester B. Pearson

My message to you all is of hope, courage and confidence. Let us mobilize all our resources in a systematic and organized way and tackle the grave issues that confront us with grim determination and discipline worthy of a great nation.

Muhammad Ali Jinnah

I've always had confidence. It came because I have lots of initiative. I wanted to make something of myself.

Eddie Murphy

I think a lot of people mistake my confidence on stage for cockiness in real life, and that's actually farthest from the truth. When I'm on stage, I'm that confident and that cocky because I have a microphone in my hand, and there's a few thousand people staring at me. And I know they're there to laugh.

Russell Peters

Regardless of how you feel inside, always try to look like a winner. Even if you are behind, a sustained look of control and confidence can give you a mental edge that results in victory.

Diane Arbus

The moment a large investor doesn't believe a government will pay back its debt when it says it will, a crisis of confidence could develop. Investors have scant patience for the years of good governance - politically fraught fiscal restructuring, austerity and debt rescheduling - it takes to defuse a sovereign-debt crisis.

Andrew Ross Sorkin

Discipline is based on pride, on meticulous attention to details, and on mutual respect and confidence. Discipline must be a habit so ingrained that it is stronger than the excitement of the goal or the fear of failure.

Gary Ryan Blair

No man has the right to dictate what other men should perceive, create or produce, but all should be encouraged to reveal themselves, their perceptions and emotions, and to build confidence in the creative spirit.

Ansel Adams

Doubt can motivate you, so don't be afraid of it. Confidence and doubt are at two ends of the scale, and you need both. They balance each other out.

Barbra Streisand

Confidence isn't optimism or pessimism, and it's not a character attribute. It's the expectation of a positive outcome.

Rosabeth Moss Kanter

As a leader, these attributes - confidence, perseverance, work ethic and good sense - are all things I look for in people. I also try to lead by example and create an environment where good questions and good ideas can come from anyone.

Heather Bresch

Besides pride, loyalty, discipline, heart, and mind, confidence is the key to all the locks.

Joe Paterno

I was not addicted to stealing in my youth, nor have ever been; yet such was the confidence of the Negroes in the neighborhood, even at this early period of my life, in my superior judgment, that they would often carry me with them when they were going on any roguery, to plan for them.

Nat Turner

I think the best way to have confidence is not to allow everyone else's insecurities to be your own.

Jessie J

I have the Midas touch, in the way that when I hook up with a project, I feel, not speaking cocky or conceited, but there's a confidence I have. I learned that from Muhammad Ali; I used to bodyguard him. He taught me about confidence. So when it comes to any job I work, I'm gonna do it good; I'm going to bring it over the top.

Mr. T

The unutterable violence of the Holocaust shook our confidence in the possibility of telling any story of faith at all.

Timothy Radcliffe

Faith is deliberate confidence in the character of God whose ways you may not understand at the time.

Oswald Chambers

Girl power is about loving yourself and having confidence and strength from within, so even if you're not wearing a sexy outfit, you feel sexy.

Nicole Scherzinger

Confidence comes from hours and days and weeks and years of constant work and dedication.

Roger Staubach

That in affairs of very considerable importance men should deal with one another with satisfaction of mind, and mutual confidence, they must receive competent assurances concerning the integrity, fidelity, and constancy each of other.

Isaac Barrow

A lot of people would say 'sexy' is about the body. But to me, 'sexy' is a woman with confidence. I admire women who have very little fear.

Allegra Versace

When you lose your hair, it has an impact on confidence

and your overall self-esteem whether it affects your career or your love life.

Bill Rancic

We need to restore the confidence in the country, first of all.

Rafik Hariri

Possessed with a full confidence of the certain success which British valor must gain over such enemies, I have led you up these steep and dangerous rocks, only solicitous to show you the foe within your reach.

James Wolfe

People who have given us their complete confidence believe that they have a right to ours. The inference is false, a gift confers no rights.

Friedrich Nietzsche

I was completely devoted to reading and books from the age of seven. It took until I was 18 to have the confidence to write poetry.

Christopher Koch

As opposed to putting too much confidence in myself, or in an image or a scene or a set of brushes, I really want to allow the oil paint to perform, to show me the things that it wants to do, beyond my imagination.

Dan Colen

I have confidence in mining. I see exciting opportunities in it.

Patrice Motsepe

At the moment we're trying to keep what we've learnt. Because we learnt a terrific amount with 'Deep Purple In Rock,' it took six months to make that album: we think it paid off, really. I can honestly say that it's the first album we've been 100 percent satisfied with; it gave us a hell of a lot of confidence.

Jon Lord

We were given clear concrete tools. The course did a great job demystifying the art of fiction writing and fostering confidence. The instructor brought complex concepts down to earth. I will miss coming here every week.

Miguel Ferrer

I have absolutely no confidence in the Ferguson police, the county prosecutor.

William Lacy Clay, Jr.

When we first went there we completely lacked confidence. Our manager told us our act was too long, and told us to drop certain numbers and concentrate on the exciting stuff. And he was right.

Steve Marriott

I knew Manuel Pellegrini from my time in Spain. I'd only heard good things about him, that he was someone who instilled the confidence in his players to go out and play good, attacking football.

Sergio Aguero

I never wanted to show my butt, and I always had a problem with it - I'd cover up when I was younger. It wasn't till I got with my husband that I started to change all that.

He compliments me all the time, and when your best friend compliments you, it gives you confidence and makes you want to do stuff in life.

Coco Austin

I was painfully shy, so my aunt suggested to my mum that me and my brother go to Stage 84, a performing arts school in Yorkshire. I've probably romanticised it in my head, but I seem to remember that in the space of an hour's drama workshop, I was transformed. I went in really shy, and I came out full of confidence.

Christian Cooke

I have full confidence in the ability of Foo Fighters' audiences to distinguish between questioning HIV and the obvious value of safe-sex practices.

Nate Mendel

You've always got to have that inner confidence in you. That's where it all starts. You're gong to have good days, you're going to have bad days. You've got to have the same desire and try to get better each day.

Scott Tolzien

I have never had feeling in my toes. My uncle, Gen. Norman Schwarzkopf, once told me in confidence he had the same syndrome, leading me to believe it is genetic.

Ethan Coen

Before the final battle in 'Poison Princess,' Evie remembered how to use her Empress powers, practiced with them to the point of exhaustion, then had a trial by fire. In a way, she earned those powers, as she hadn't before, so that was certainly a confidence builder.

Kresley Cole

If somebody says they are going to do something - and then later they don't - it affects me a lot, and I lose confidence in them.

Royston Drenthe

I've dated girls that aren't, this is gonna sound so horrible, that aren't super smart, but they still are super confident, and that's more what I've been attracted to is the confidence and the sense of humor.

Parker Young

The first entry into modeling doesn't build your confidence. They pull out the tape measure and pick you apart. I'm a curvy woman, so I was definitely told I was 'too curvy.'

Joelle Carter

I am disposed to be thus particular from the interest you take in our welfare and from the entire confidence I have in your knowing, that you will be sympathetic with us in our misfortunes.

John Hawley

The challenge of directing and interviewing helped me with confidence, and I learnt so much. If I hadn't had the brain hemorrhage, I might never have done it.

Maryam D'Abo

You can be chased home or hit or called names or spit on, and it's over. You have the memory of it, but it's very different from the emotional and psychological experience of feeling invisible, of not learning the confidence to stand up in class and speak.

Chirlane McCray

A good ground rule for writing in any genre is, start with a form, then undermine its confidence in itself. Ask what it's afraid of, what it's trying to hide - then write that.

M. John Harrison

Human spirit is the ability to face the uncertainty of the future with curiosity and optimism. It is the belief that problems can be solved, differences resolved. It is a type of confidence. And it is fragile. It can be blackened by fear and superstition.

Bernard Beckett

I don't even know how to speak up for myself, because I don't really have a father who would give me the confidence or advice. And if you're always the new kid, you never get a chance to adapt, so your confidence is just zilch.

Eminem

Action is a great restorer and builder of confidence. Inaction is not only the result, but the cause, of fear. Perhaps the action you take will be successful; perhaps different action or adjustments will have to follow. But any action is better than no action at all.

Norman Vincent Peale

If once you forfeit the confidence of your fellow-citizens, you can never regain their respect and esteem.

Abraham Lincoln

Just what future the Designer of the universe has provided for the souls of men I do not know, I cannot prove. But I find that the whole order of Nature confirms my confidence that, if it is not like our noblest hopes and dreams, it will transcend them.

Henry Norris Russell

Honesty is the cornerstone of all success, without which confidence and ability to perform shall cease to exist.

Mary Kay Ash

Whatever we expect with confidence becomes our own self-fulfilling prophecy.

Brian Tracy

If you're in a workplace you don't like right now, be encouraged because God will use it for your good. Think about it this way: He wants you to be a light in the darkness - and He's putting His confidence in you!

Joyce Meyer

All you need is ignorance and confidence and the success is sure.

Mark Twain

I tremble for my country when I hear of confidence expressed in me. I know too well my weakness, that our only hope is in God.

Robert E. Lee

It's a deep and all but certain truth about narcissistic personalities that to meet them is to love them, but to know them well is to find them unbearable. Confidence quickly curdles into arrogance; smarts turn to smugness, charm turns to smarm.

Jeffrey Kluger

Whether you come from a council estate or a country estate, your success will be determined by your own confidence and fortitude.

Michelle Obama

The people no longer has confidence in its former protectors, now its exploiters and executioners. The masks have fallen.

Jose Rizal

Confidence is the most important single factor in this game, and no matter how great your natural talent, there is only one way to obtain and sustain it: work.

Jack Nicklaus

I have a large watch collection, and classic watches are especially important to me. I had a silver Rolex, and I actually gave it to my little brother. He wears it every day. He's an actor, so whenever he goes to an audition, he can look down, see it, and it gives him confidence. It was a great thing to pass on.

Nate Berkus

I thought I'd be edgy and dye my hair red. And I dyed my hair, like, Jessica Rabbit red. It kind of allowed me to have this whole new confidence and this whole new swagger and this whole new sense of self. It kind of brought out the inner rock star in me. I had never dyed my hair like that, and no one forgot me after that.

Candice Accola

The greater the artist, the greater the doubt. Perfect confidence is granted to the less talented as a consolation prize.

Robert Hughes

One of the jobs of a manager is to instill confidence, pump confidence into your people. And when you've got somebody who's raring to go and you can smell it and feel it, give 'em that shot.

Jack Welch

But by reading them again and again finally I was able to grasp the essential part. What emotion, enthusiasm, enlightenment and confidence they communicated to me! I wept for joy.

Ho Chi Minh

Everyone has ideas. They may be too busy or lack the confidence or technical ability to carry them out. But I want to carry them out. It is a matter of getting up and doing it.

James Dyson

I place no hope in my strength, nor in my works: but all my confidence is in God my protector, who never abandons those who have put all their hope and thought in him.

Francois Rabelais

Confidence is a lot of this game or any game. If you don't think you can, you won't.

Jerry West

I know I can be bolshy and really unpleasant, and it always happens if I lose confidence in the people I'm working with. If I've got no confidence in what I'm doing and they don't provide me with some assurance that we're doing the right thing then I bully people. I'm a horrible bully.

Kristin Scott Thomas

A lot of the motivation for doing the 'Make 'Em Laugh' on SNL was because I had just finished shooting 'Inception,' where there were zero-gravity scenes and I got into really good shape and was training and did all these stunts. Coming off of that, that instilled me with the confidence to do 'Make 'Em Laugh.'

Joseph Gordon-Levitt

He who closes his ears to the views of others shows little confidence in the integrity of his own views.

William Congreve

If you got a good imagination, a lot of confidence and you kind of know what you are saying, then you might be able to do it. I know a lot of colorful characters at home that would make great actors.

Jason Statham

When you win, you don't get carried away. But if you go step by step, with confidence, you can go far.

Diego Maradona

I am concerned about any attrition in customer traffic at Starbucks, but I don't want to use the economy, commodity prices or consumer confidence as an excuse. We must maintain a value proposition to our customers as well as differentiate the Starbucks Experience. That is the key.

Howard Schultz

Love means that everything is right with the world. Love and only love. Love means that you are content within your own heart and in the presence of the person that you love, who fills your day and makes you stronger and wiser, and gives you the confidence to go out into the world. Love is just the most beautiful, joyous feeling.

Pierce Brosnan

Pixar's short films convinced Disney that if the company could produce memorable characters within five minutes, then the confidence was there in creating a feature film with those abilities in story and character development.

John Lasseter

I am strong-willed, which can be annoying sometimes. And from that I think people assume I have confidence and

Hollywood glamour and all that stuff, when actually, in my personal life, sometimes I'm just a goofball.

Catherine Zeta-Jones

I know people who've had a nose job, and they've walked out feeling a million dollars, and their confidence is tenfold. Good on them! Natural beauty comes in all different shapes and sizes, but if you think surgery would right something you have a problem with, then why shouldn't you do it?

Louise Nurding

As a direct line to human feeling, empathic experience, genuine language and detail, poetry is everything that headline news is not. It takes us inside situations, helps us imagine life from more than one perspective, honors imagery and metaphor - those great tools of thought - and deepens our confidence in a meaningful world.

Naomi Shihab Nye

When you look good, you feel good. Confidence with what you're wearing is very important. If you feel good, you will always perform your best without worrying about anything.

Maria Sharapova

At a young age winning is not the most important thing...
the important thing is to develop creative and skilled
players with good confidence.

Arsene Wenger

I'm always impressed by confidence, kindness and a sense
of humour.

Tamara Mellon

Being deeply knowledgeable on one subject narrows one's
focus and increases confidence, but it also blurs dissenting
views until they are no longer visible, thereby transforming
data collection into bias confirmation and morphing self-
deception into self-assurance.

Michael Shermer

A good education gives you confidence to stick up your
hand for anything - whether it is the job you want, or the
bloke. And the more you stick up your hand, the better your
chances are that you will get what you want.

Kate Reardon

I'm currently single, so I want to have fun! As for what guys need to do to date out of their league, it's all about the swagger. If you have confidence, you can get pretty much any girl.

Krysten Ritter

Listen, if you don't talk big game, you never get anywhere. If you don't think big, you don't get big. Some people call it egotistical, some people call it high hopes, some people call it confidence. It's all in how you want to dissect it.

Vanilla Ice

If my parents were still alive, they would be very proud. They gave me a good start in life, the values that have driven me, and the confidence to believe in myself.

Alex Ferguson

You've got to take the initiative and play your game. In a decisive set, confidence is the difference.

Chris Evert

Confidence is a very fragile thing.

Joe Montana

At the beginning of a novel, a writer needs confidence, but after that what's required is persistence. These traits sound similar. They aren't. Confidence is what politicians, seducers, and currency speculators have, but persistence is a quality found in termites. It's the blind drive to keep on working that persists after confidence breaks down.

Walter Kirn

When we have done our best, we can, as a united people, take whatever may befall with calm courage and confidence that this old nation will survive and if death should come to many of us, death is not the end.

Eamon de Valera

The definition of swagger, in my opinion, is you have to have that arrogance, that confidence that you are the best out there at all times.

Keyshawn Johnson

Unless someone wants to look funny, I'll not recommend anyone to copy my bowling action. But on a serious note, with the confidence that I have got from the amount of runs I have been scoring, when I'm thrown the ball to bowl, I am pretty sure of what I have to do. I may not be the most attractive to watch while bowling, but I can be effective.

Virat Kohli

And I might add the confidence with which distracted persons do oftentimes, when they are awake, think, they see black fiends in places, where there is no black object in sight without them.

Robert Boyle

When you give a lot of confidence in people and you don't get it back, you are a bit disappointed, but it's life.

Carine Roitfeld

It is not so much our friends' help that helps us, as the confidence of their help.

Epicurus

The trust of the people in the leaders reflects the confidence of the leaders in the people.

Paulo Freire

As a young boy, scouting gave me a confidence and camaraderie that is hard to find in modern life.

Bear Grylls

There is no worse screen to block out the Spirit than confidence in our own intelligence.

John Calvin

I love the confidence that makeup gives me.

Tyra Banks

Kids made fun of me because I was a slow learner, because I was hyperactive, because of a lot of things. Running gave me confidence.

Steve Prefontaine

I haven't experienced love at first sight yet. I've seen very, very beautiful girls and been awestruck but never love at first sight. I think confidence goes such a long way with women. A girl who is confident with who she is and she can really flaunt that is really sexy.

Tristan Wilds

He who has faith has... an inward reservoir of courage, hope, confidence, calmness, and assuring trust that all will come out well - even though to the world it may appear to come out most badly.

B. C. Forbes

Analysis gave me great freedom of emotions and fantastic confidence. I felt I had served my time as a puppet.

Hedy Lamarr

Fighters display two things. They display confidence, or they display a look that says, 'I'm not sure.'

Sugar Ray Leonard

The great gift of Easter is hope - Christian hope which

makes us have that confidence in God, in his ultimate triumph, and in his goodness and love, which nothing can shake.

Basil Hume

It is only prudent never to place complete confidence in that by which we have even once been deceived.

Rene Descartes

There is a difference between conceit and confidence. Conceit is bragging about yourself. Confidence means you believe you can get the job done.

Johnny Unitas

Your teammates give you the confidence. They give me the confidence all year, all postseason.

LeBron James

Confidence is that feeling by which the mind embarks in great and honorable courses with a sure hope and trust in itself.

Marcus Tullius Cicero

Confidence is very sexy. You could be not cute at all and have such confidence.

Kirsten Dunst

Success produces confidence; confidence relaxes industry, and negligence ruins the reputation which accuracy had raised.

Ben Jonson

Enhancing a woman's silhouette and enhancing a woman's beauty - both contribute to enhancing her confidence, so they're synonymous, really.

L'Wren Scott

Courage is a mean with regard to fear and confidence.

Aristotle

Confidence in the goodness of another is good proof of one's own goodness.

Michel de Montaigne

If in preaching the gospel you substitute your knowledge of the way of salvation for confidence in the power of the gospel, you hinder people from getting to reality.

Oswald Chambers

I often find it's just the confidence that makes you sexy, not what your body looks like. It's how you feel about yourself that makes you sexy.

Queen Latifah

I think the most important thing about coaching is that you have to have a sense of confidence about what you're doing.

Phil Jackson

A decent government with an effective, but not gratuitously violent, police force and a fair court system are essential. This deters and incapacitates psychopaths, bullies and hotheads - and if it earns the confidence of the people, they don't have to become violent in self-defence.

Steven Pinker

Unfortunately, corruption is widespread in government agencies and public enterprises. Our political system promotes nepotism and wasting money. This has undermined our legal system and confidence in the functioning of the state. One of the consequences is that many citizens don't pay their taxes.

George Papandreou

You tell your kids that no matter what, you set your goals and you go for them. Whatever it is you achieve, never give up. You want your kids to have that good attitude, the confidence, and the will power to believe in themselves.

Joel Parkinson

If a man has been his mother's undisputed darling he retains throughout life the triumphant feeling, the confidence in success, which not seldom brings actual success along with it.

Sigmund Freud

There's a line that separates having confidence and being conceited. I don't cross that line, but I have a lot of confidence in myself.

Paul Pierce

In a war everybody always knows all about Switzerland, in peace times it is just Switzerland but in war time it is the only country that everybody has confidence in, everybody.

Gertrude Stein

Intuition is the wisdom formed by feeling and instinct - a gift of knowing without reasoning... Belief is ignited by hope and supported by facts and evidence - it builds alignment and creates confidence. Belief is what sets energy in motion and creates the success that breeds more success.

Angela Ahrendts

I've had confidence in myself all along. It was just a matter of getting the pieces back in place.

Dale Earnhardt

If we focus on our health, including our inner health, our self-esteem, and how we look at ourselves and our confidence level, we'll tend to be healthier people anyway, we'll tend to make better choices for our lives, for our bodies, we'll always be trying to learn more, and get better as time goes on.

Queen Latifah

I know what it's like to feel that fear and the need of affirmation and appreciation. To build confidence in yourself is the toughest thing.

Shakira

The people have given me their support; they have given me their trust and confidence. My colleagues have suffered a lot in order to give me support. I do not look upon my life as a sacrifice at all.

Aung San Suu Kyi

There is all this controversy that women and girls are too skinny or too overweight. I say to just do martial arts and everything will be okay. You will tone up your body and find a confidence you can't find just sitting around watching TV and hanging out with friends.

Milla Jovovich

Only one man ever betrayed my confidence, and that only in a minor matter.

Harry Houdini

I think confidence is the sexiest thing to have.

Jessie J

It's been a dream of mine to run my own summer camp. I went to one as a kid, and I put on productions, and got lots of confidence.

Idina Menzel

I think naturally, if you're an actor, there's a high level of assertiveness that you need to have to survive this business. There's boldness in being assertive, and there's strength and confidence.

Bryan Cranston

Confidence is everything in this business.

Reese Witherspoon

The negative aspects of Scottish Nationalism are a kind of aggressive complacency, that sort of boasting; but that's an expression of insecurity, I think, of a lack of confidence.

Douglas Dunn

I don't have the confidence to pull off a moustache.

Rich Sommer

My habit would have been to veer towards the dark - to prove I was something; edgy, or maybe to prove that I was cognisant of the dark side. Now, with age and confidence, I can say, yeah, that's true, but I am cognisant of the fact that people can do things well. And can be more loving than you expect.

George Saunders

When I realised I had a facility for humour, I latched on to it, and it gave me confidence and I built my personality around it. So I subconsciously made myself become the funny one so that would be my label rather than the ginger one or the red-faced one.

Catherine Tate

The man of genius inspires us with a boundless confidence in our own powers.

Ralph Waldo Emerson

Peace comes when you talk to the guy you most hate. And that's where the courage of a leader comes, because when you sit down with your enemy, you as a leader must already have very considerable confidence from your own constituency.

Desmond Tutu

To walk around with an ego is a bad thing. To have confidence in yourself is a great thing.

Fred Durst

Confidence in others' honesty is no light testimony of one's own integrity.

Michel de Montaigne

Conceit is bragging about yourself. Confidence means you believe you can get the job done.

Johnny Unitas

Oh, how great peace and quietness would he possess who should cut off all vain anxiety and place all his confidence in God.

Thomas a Kempis

You have to have confidence in your ability, and then be tough enough to follow through.

Rosalynn Carter

You need to play with supreme confidence, or else you'll lose again, and then losing becomes a habit.

Joe Paterno

Confidence is key. Sometimes, you need to look like you're confident even when you're not.

Vanessa Hudgens

Beauty is grace and confidence. I've learned to accept and appreciate what nature gave me.

Lindsay Lohan

Confidence is at the root of so many attractive qualities, a sense of humor, a sense of style, a willingness to be who you are no matter what anyone else might think or say and it's true, I do have a certain fondness for women that have dark hair.

Wentworth Miller

I've always been attracted to women who are assertive and have confidence - qualities older women possess. They've been on the Earth a little longer. They're more seasoned. They don't play games. They know what they want, and they're not afraid to tell you.

Taye Diggs

In all my public and private acts as your president, I expect to follow my instincts of openness and candor with full confidence that honesty is always the best policy in the end.

Gerald R. Ford

It has been my privilege on various occasions to converse with presidents of the United States and important men in other governments. At the close of each such occasion, I have reflected on the rewarding experience of standing with confidence in the presence of an acknowledged leader.

Gordon B. Hinckley

Confidence. If you have it, you can make anything look good.

Diane von Furstenberg

But the world is ever more interdependent. Stock markets and economies rise and fall together. Confidence is the key to prosperity. Insecurity spreads like contagion. So people crave stability and order.

Tony Blair

Confidence, as a teenager? Because I knew what I loved. I loved to read; I loved to listen to music; and I loved cats. Those three things. So, even though I was an only kid, I could be happy because I knew what I loved.

Haruki Murakami

Concentration comes out of a combination of confidence and hunger.

Arnold Palmer

Style is the instrument you can pick back up when you want to regain some of the confidence you've lost.

Stacy London

If you have money and you have fame, but you don't have any confidence in your blackness, then it's all for nothing.

Paul Mooney

Like the rest of the genetic lottery, beauty is unfair. Everyone falls short of perfection, but some are luckier than others. Real confidence requires self-knowledge, which includes recognizing one's shortcomings as well as one's strengths.

Virginia Postrel

Relaxing at home in his 55th-floor condominium before a game, Sammy Sosa is the same as at the ball park: focused but funny, exuberant but reserved. He is in a strange country, conversing in two languages, but his every movement displays a combination of confidence and humility.

Bill Dedman

The only thing that I can do is know that I have great confidence in raising children and being a great mother.

Cheryl Tiegs

I like looking feminine and I enjoy being a role model. I enjoy being a woman. It all comes down to having the confidence to be who you are.

Cathy Freeman

It is the parent's job to see how their child learns and to make sure that the children's self confidence is buoyed at all times, or they will plummet like a stone.

Henry Winkler

The way you delegate is that first you have to hire people that you really have confidence in. You won't truly let those people feel a sense of autonomy if you don't have confidence in them.

Robert Pozen

I remember, when I went away to college at Southern

Methodist University in Dallas, my aunt sent me a book with the rules of being a Southern Belle. One of the rules was to never wear white after Labor Day. Fashion has a lot to do with confidence and making up your own rules.

Kourtney Kardashian

I think it takes a lot of confidence to be comfortable in being vulnerable.

Ciara

There has not been a war in South America for fifty years, and I have every confidence that the countries of Central and South America are deeply in earnest in the maintenance of peace.

Frank B. Kellogg

Confidence is a plant of slow growth in an aged heart.

William Pitt

Playing in the playoffs is the best basketball in the world, and if you can learn under that pressure, succeed under that pressure, it gives you more confidence the next year.

Tony Parker

Whatever it is that gives you that confidence will vary from person to person, but I do believe that it is the key to succeeding at anything in life - career, relationships, anything.

Molly Ringwald